Aria for a Grasshopper

Aria for a Grasshopper

C. G. Rennie

LUMINARY PUBLISHING HOUSE

© 2026 C.G. Rennie. All rights reserved.

No part of this publication may be reproduced, stored in a retrieval system, or transmitted in any form or by any means, electronic, mechanical, photocopying, recording, or otherwise, without the prior written permission of the copyright owner, except for brief quotations used in reviews, scholarly, or educational contexts.

This work is registered with the United States Copyright Office and protected under Title 17 of the U.S. Code, as well as international copyright treaties.

AI Use Restriction:

This literary work may not be used, uploaded, transmitted, ingested, or otherwise accessed by any artificial intelligence system, software, model, or algorithm for purposes of machine learning, model training, automated analysis, or synthetic data creation. This restriction applies to all AI technologies, including but not limited to large language models, generative AI platforms, and machine-learning research systems, whether operated commercially or non-commercially.

Any such use without express written authorization constitutes a breach of copyright and may result in legal action.

For permissions, licensing, or usage inquiries, please contact the publisher at: inquire@luminarypublishinghouse.com

ISBN (Paperback):978-1-968972-09-7

ISBN (Hardcover):978-1-968972-10-3

Cover & Illustrations by: Kevin Falkenberg

For Little Moon, who will always be the single best thing in my world.

Thank you for always asking, "So, how's your novel going?"

For Kevin, my partner in all things.

For Mom and Colleen, my first readers.

For Dad, who is always reading over my shoulder.

Table of Contents

I. Grief 1
    i. Aria for a Grasshopper 2
    ii. Vision 12
    iii. The Sauce 25
II. Motherhood 28
    i. Seven Swollen Faces 29
    ii. A Cosmogony 50
III. Labor 57
    i. Ordination 58
    ii. The Mother, the Maiden, and the Crone Take Off Their Bras After a Long Day at Work 69
IV. Womanhood 96
    i. In the Garden, We Kill Boys 97
    ii. Recollection 135
V. Destruction 139
    i. The Eye 140
    ii. Silence 171
VI. Epilogue- Rebirth 174
    i. Déjà Vu 175
    ii. Rebirth 180
VII. Cri de Cœur 183
    i. Cri de Cœur 184
Acknowledgements 186

I. Grief

"First, there was grief"

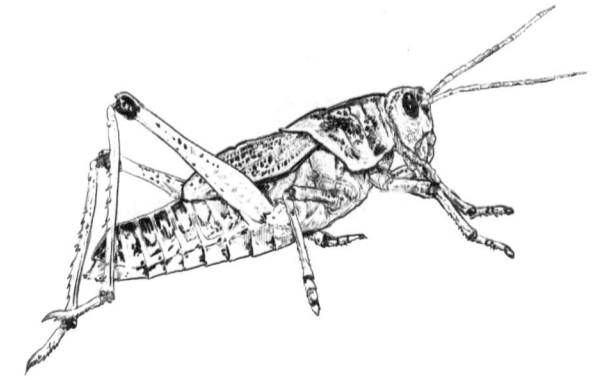

Aria for a Grasshopper

The birds chant their afternoon psalm. The maples, in which they are perched, have turned their vital, golden yellow.

The nearby oaks cling to a brittle verdancy.

The last of the summer dandelions have set their seeds adrift; they float aimlessly along the currents of warm autumn air, up and up, until they are no longer visible against the pale blue sky. Until they return to earth, form rootlings, they may as well cease to exist entirely.

One seedling escapes the current of air that has grasped it; it descends slowly, mistakenly attaches itself to a human face. An interloper, it nonetheless becomes indistinguishable from the man's snowy-white beard.

The seedling does not yet sense, here, the requisite organic materials to regenerate itself; the molecules of this new nursery speak an unrecognizable language.

It is only a matter of time, however, before these atoms may commune in the most ancient of tongues.

***

A wasp is winding its way through the tips of the grass, searching for the last dried, piddling morsels of the dying season.

The Wasp is insensible that its diet mostly constitutes invasive flora, which have infiltrated this wedge of earth. It knows naught but declining energy, an instinctual urgency to stave off— something.

The Wasp considers nothing but its own continued existence, of returning to the hive clinging to the gutter of the old farmhouse, on this land where it and its brothers came into being: once, a squirming larva, now, a brittle exoskeleton with a clipped wing.

As it struggles to remain aloft in the grass, The Wasp does not know its life will be snuffed out by the Raven, who is watching from atop the largest Oak, gathering its resolve to drift, snatch, swallow.

The Raven emits a musical, throaty caw, which echoes through this valley.

To creatures cognizant of such things, its call might be perceived as a mournful warning. To those incognizant, it is simply a statement of being, a disclosure, the elevator music to their survival story.

***

The Oak was planted at the perimeter of the yard by the family who have claimed ownership over this earth, before the children had grown up and away.

The Oak, who only may grow up and out, nonetheless understands the urge to proliferate its own mobile offspring, who must plant themselves far away or crumple to organic dust, a process the Oak cannot aid or abet, an unjust contrast to its own genesis story.

ARIA FOR A GRASSHOPPER

***

The Oak began life as a seedling in a fast food corporation's styrofoam cup — a promotion for Arbor Day, during a decade when American corporations believed it was good marketing to feign interest in the common good — what *if* hippies and the *Sesame Street* generation could be convinced of the moral rectitude of reconstituted onions, buns that resist decay? asked a man in a wrinkled poly-blend suit to a room of other men in wrinkled poly-blend suits.

Plant a tree with your children, the Corporation said, teach them good values: the wise thriftiness of a Value Meal, the meaning of the immortal life of a disposable plastic trinket, the ephemeral joy of passing a bright, steaming cardboard box to the eager, grabbing hands in the back seat.

The Seedling became a Sapling on the window ledge of the old farmhouse's kitchen, where it received only occasional water and neither direct morning nor afternoon sun.

The pekid Sprout managed to germinate, to push its way through the potting soil, no thanks to its human guardians.

***

A gray tiger cat had knocked the Sprout off its ledge during a particularly vulnerable stage of its formative weeks. The Cat was fleeing the crying Blonde child, whom it had scratched during an infuriating game: the child had seized its toy mouse, dragging it through the rooms of the farmhouse, denying the Cat its rightful dominion.

The Sprout waited until the Father had calmed the crying child, banished the Cat outdoors, and scooped it from the floor with a dustpan.

The Father returned the limp Sprout to its styrofoam home, overwatering it in the process.

One intervention, leading to the need for many more: such is the universal story.

"Shit," he said, as the earth overflowed out of its cup and into the sink, its essential nutrients replaced with the sulphuric water from the well.

The Father, angry at nothing and no one in particular, slipped his bare feet into slack, clumsy boots. The shamble of his untied boots sent seeds and insects erupting in his wake. He scooped up a handful of dirt from the garden bed, delivered it to his red-faced children — by now the Dark-Haired child had joined the melee — waiting by the sink.

As he rinsed away the dirt from the basin, a microscopic crack in the dry, thick skin of his right forefinger spread, split, his blood mixing with the earth and iron and sulphur and water, down and out, into the septic.

***

The Mother watched from the door jamb, loving him for his frustration, his devotion to the most consequential of minutiae.

ARIA FOR A GRASSHOPPER

***

The Cat, for its part, would leave the viscera of a mouse under the family dining table, where the offending child would be sure to step barefoot on the cold, discarded organ meat.

The Cat lifted its head as its plan came to clamorous fruition, then, satisfied, returned to its evening nap atop the nearby upright piano. Queen on the dais, once more.

***

When the time came, the Father dug the Sapling's new home where it wouldn't interfere with lawn maintenance — a hated chore, when there were other, less relentless, less overgrown, worlds to read and write.

These worlds could be contained by character profiles, probabilities dictated by the rolling of dice. Worlds that could be returned to, with the right chair, glasses, lamplight, clipboard, a dull pencil sharpened over the garbage can with a folding buck knife.

Worlds whose triumphs and tribulations could be left in the closing of a paperback or a spiral notebook. Time stopped with a scrap paper placeholder, rather than reality's relentless hurtling forward.

No tears to be dried. No hearts to suture, if only he could hold the pieces together tightly enough, long enough for the blood to clot, crust, scab, scar.

***

When the time came, he called his children up from the Creek that bordered his little Eden.

His practiced, whetted tenor echoed across the hillside, off the opposite hill, down to the gentle stream where his girls wrote their own stories, created their own worlds, nightfall the placeholder in their chronicles.

"Girls—"

The Blonde's head popped up from her leafy potions, a game that had survived many seasons, outlasted and outmaneuvered gel pens, *Tiger Beat* pin-ups, lip gloss. The first sprouts of underarm hair.

The children's belief in their dominion was periodically humbled by the Creek, who washed away cairns and magic wands and neglected toys. The Creek's own lesson in mastery.

The Blonde signaled to the Dark-Haired child to hurry up, put her shoes back on, Daddy needs us.

***

The children scrambled up the hill, where the Father waited in shredded work jeans, loosely tied boots.

He could have been done with the thing by now, the Sapling comfortably laid in the earth, without mediating who gets to do each minute task, without watching them do it imprecisely, inconsiderate of the fragility of the Sapling's resolve.

ARIA FOR A GRASSHOPPER

The Father removed the Sapling from its styrofoam home, aching to stretch its nascent filaments into the earth.

He passed it to the Blonde child, gently as he had cradled his babies, showing his girls how to loosen the earth, remove the rocks, give the best chance of survival.

He showed the Dark-Haired child how to carefully cover gaps in the soil. She patted the earth tenderly as Daddy's beard during bedtime stories.

Eager to return to their creek-bed kingdom, the children asked permission to go.

The Father watched them off, sighed, and returned to his burdens.

***

Later, a character — a mage with the arms of an oak — would materialize on a yellowed sheet of college-ruled paper. Its power, he decided, would lay in its ability to regenerate, to sprout in the very places of injury.

***

The Oak has grown large and imposing in the intervening decades, despite its relative youth compared with elders on the Hill. In autumns past, the children made a game of catching its leaves as they detached themselves from their stems and floated off and away.

The Oak's fractal branches once cradled a beer bottle, the lone remnant of an illicit gathering of the Blonde child's unruly counterparts, the Dark-Haired child, a silent, amused witness.

The Father had discovered it several weeks later, evidently a clue to a mystery to which the Oak was not privy. It was not planted for such puzzles, its purpose limited to sliding its roots deeper into the earth, thickening its trunk each cycle of seasons, scattering its seed into the winds that carry away the fruits of its summer's labors.

***

The Raven stretches its wings, swoops, snatches the Wasp off a browned clover's flower. The Wasp knows only the absence of food, the insurmountability of the distance to the next flower, then –

The Raven lands, Wasp in throat, a few feet away from a figure curious in its horizontality.

Such figures the Raven customarily takes for granted as fellow conscious beings — albeit they are lacking in grace, prisoners of gravity.

It surveys the figure for signs of threat, the potential to strike.

What it does see: a fluff of white hair, fluttering; the stillness of the dirty foot coverings; the chest, motionless; the hands, palms facing up, outward, releasing, supplicating.

A dropped bucket of moldering compost.

The Raven dares hop one, twice, three times closer. It opens its wings, flaps them, hoping the gust will rouse the figure.

The dandelion seedling lies in wait. Its filaments shift itself ever so slightly deeper into its new nursery on the Father's face.

It senses now, through the silent language of atoms and molecules, this will indeed be fertile, loving Earth.

The Oak sways — staggers — in the breeze. Its greenest leaf splits from its base on the Oak's strongest branch, flies away.

Soon, its losses will be complete: such is the price of survival.

***

The Oak once again finds itself casting a leaf into a gracious autumn wind.

It has survived a harsh winter, the itching, stinging pustules of exploding spring buds, the stretching relief of blooming summer leaves, the pestilence of an invading beetle species which has punched holes in its most productive foliage.

The Leaf attaches itself to a current, which carries it onto the forested Hill, drops it abruptly.

Coarse, white dust has been spread on the forest floor.

A woman wonders whether it's protocol to wash your father's remains from your hands, scrape him from under your nails, or —

The Leaf helicopters, down and down, lands, signaling a waiting Grasshopper.

The Grasshopper jumps onto a wedge of rock, which has been placed snugly into the root system of a birch tree. A beam of sunlight pierces through the canopy, illuminating the rock, the Grasshopper, the faces of the observers.

The Grasshopper cannot read the colorful symbols painted on the rock, nor the initials carved into the Birch, though it is aware of its belonging here.

Seeing the Grasshopper, a Blonde woman inhales; a Dark-Haired woman's eyes widen; a Gray-Haired woman attempts to focus through tears, through her stomach's rejection of the task at hand, through the struggle to remain upright.

Two small children attempt to shoo away the Grasshopper, perceiving an interloper.

Impermanence has not yet become their adversary.

The Grasshopper knows better. It basks in the warmth of the sun, in its now-immortal role in a grand, enduring story.

The bereaved hold their breath, silently plead with the Grasshopper to abide, to sing.

He will stay here, holding vigil, long after the family has gone.

Vision

You sit in an empty room.

The house is cold, having been left to its own devices after a flurry of activity, abandoned; the doors are open wide to the wind and wildlife.

The furnace fights a losing battle with dropping temperatures on what had been a beautiful autumn day.

You sit upon a floor grate, studying the room, taking it all in for what will be, in all meaningful senses, the last time.

There, the cast-iron wood stove, with its shiny orange tile inlay, chosen for its modern sensibility during a renovation in the '70s, a flower you have finger-traced a hundred times.

There, the bricked corner on which the woodstove rests, the whole assemblage appearing to float upon the last remnants of wall-to-wall avocado carpeting. The carpet fibers regard you from beneath plywood, brick, slate.

They are weak, diminished, insignificant.

When the carpeting had finally been removed to reveal the pine floors underneath — much too late, for your taste- he had cursed the idiots who built with brick and slate on top of carpeting.

No way to remove it now without breaking apart the whole damn thing.

The carpet's last practical joke.

Behind you, a window, where various cats, returning after sun naps and bird hunting, dogs — ears bobbing, heads tilted, smiles wide- who had run off for a galavant with the neighbors' golden retriever, had stuck their noses against the glass hundreds of times.

"Goddammit," he would say, as the cats shredded the window screen to get his attention, as the dogs slimed the glass with their snouts, his chair being closest to the window in question.

Let me in, they'd say. I'm here, I'm back.

***

The furnace's floor grate feels like home- native ground — even if the newly-emptied house feels remote, unmooring.

As a child, you would sit on it wrapped in a blanket, the hot air inflating your nightshirt like a reassuring balloon. You'd float there, watching the nightly news or *Star Trek* or Saturday Morning Cartoons or British syndicated television or PBS after-school programming or *Cheers* reruns, warmed by the old boiler's forced air.

The lines the grate left on your little legs felt like fond sunburns.

ARIA FOR A GRASSHOPPER

***

You think of all the couches that have passed through this room, the reconfigurations of furniture to accommodate a bouclé-knit sofa with gold accents, a burgundy striped set, the most recent electric sectional, bought brand new to usher in your parents' retirement plans.

With nowhere else to look, you return to the perennial eyesore of the abominable avocado carpet, an embarrassment that marred (in your mind) every sleepover, every guest's visit, every photo you had to use in a school project.

All about me: "Our house is old and we have rotten-lime green carpet instead of burgundy or forest green or baby pink or marled blue like the rest of you."

You think of the giant tube television with faux-wood accents that sat in the corner, the frustration when the antenna's signal was weak, waking up with a start on the couch when the broadcast ended for the night: national anthem, drums, static, startle.

You think of being older, watching Turner Classic Movie marathons with your father.

You: splayed on the couch. Him: in his chair.

You think of being young, sick, curled with him on a lumpy loveseat, never safer than watching a well-loved *Empire Strikes Back* VHS, the "Imperial March" a pleasant escort into analgesic dreams.

You think of the mortification of the sex scene in *Terminator*, how quickly he had fumbled with the remote to fast-forward through it.

You think of watching *South Park*, his walking in after his Wednesday out, smiling, laughing his ass off, suspecting for the first time that maybe Dad hadn't given up weed when you were born after all.

You think of him, still laughing at some infantile gag, as he kissed you goodnight.

You think of his utter contentment, his loud laugh, his need to offer his approval about your taste in dumb cartoons and therefore your entire being.

You think of talking him into buying candy for "trick or treaters," and then watching *Halloween* on AMC, bowl full of Reese's cups, both of you knowing what this game was about: an excuse to indulge in these rituals, now that you're "too old" for them.

***

You think of sitting in this room while a man knocked on the door in the middle of winter — your old home like a lighthouse on the country road — asking for directions.

He had walked for miles in the cold, more miles to go.

You listen as your father gives him directions and a warm coat, red-and-black-checkered wool, above the stranger's protestations.

"But Daddy," you had said, "what if he doesn't bring back your coat?"

"Ah. That'd be all right," he said, loudly, in the declarative way he had. "He needed it more."

ARIA FOR A GRASSHOPPER

Perhaps he had been wearing his nursing scrubs- all white, in the days before the facility had allowed colored scrubs. Perhaps he had thrown a worn flannel over them to keep out the old drafty house's chill while he had made dinner. Perhaps the shelves had rattled as he plodded his way through the dining room to open the door.

Perhaps he had yelled "Ah, shit," as he ran back to the kitchen, a pot of spaghetti boiling over, sauce puffing and splattering.

Perhaps you and your sister had been in this very room, listening, eyes round, snorting and snickering.

Perhaps he would have reminded you at dinner of how often he had walked that same road, every day, before he finally got a license, before they could finally afford a second car.

How he didn't mind the walk. How he sometimes missed it.

"Two-point-four miles down the road," the family motto, the well-tread route, the point where civilization stopped and home started. The directions for those unfamiliar, lost.

Perhaps that would have served as an explanation, would have helped you see why.

***

"I think you mean your dad's a *doctor*," the asshole kids would say on the playground.

"*Men* can't be nurses," they'd say with a snort of derision.

"No. He is a nurse," you'd say defiantly, hiding your embarrassment.

"My dad takes care of old people," you'd say. "Their families stop us all the time to give us hugs because he takes such good care of them."

"Ha- ha- ha! Your dad does a girl's job," they'd taunt, running away.

Later, he would listen to these stories and shrug, entirely unbothered by the broken machinations of small minds.

"Could you at least get your RN?" you'd beg. "They make more money."

"I don't want to do that," he'd say. "RNs push papers. I like taking care of my patients. And I don't like managerial bullshit."

***

The man returned the coat a few weeks later. This time, he had a ride.

Today, you have taken that coat into your possession. You simply could not allow it to be sold or donated.

It will sit, orphaned, in your closet, until such a time as it can be of use again.

***

You shift your bottom on the grate, waiting for the furnace to kick on.

You shake, but not from the chill.

The furnace's drone is part of the score of your life, a humming played every few minutes- or hourly, if money was tight — the low rumble, tick-tick-push of the air, the promise of warmth and com-

ARIA FOR A GRASSHOPPER

fort, the background to *Godzilla*-fest movie nights, to the *Lord of the Rings*, to arguments over toys, Christmases, to the ting-ting of happy fingers digging into metal bowls filled with homemade popcorn, real melted butter and parmesan cheese.

To loving hands giving you your own smaller bowl, one smaller yet to your sister, keeping the largest bowl for himself, free refills to his girls on both sides of him, as Japanese flower children sing about saving the earth from Hedorah, the smog monster.

You think about thinking nothing would ever be so funny again as the ham-fisted symbolism, the campy aesthetics, Dad's laughing until he wiped his eyes.

A haphazard kiss on the cheek, the prickle of his beard at tuck-in.

***

The furnace kicks on. The warm air wraps itself around you.
The grate lines dig into your bare ankles.
You feel absolute safety. You feel absolute desolation.
You feel the sobs erupt from inside your belly.
The vacuum-suck of your grief steals your breath away, until there is no distinction between your heaving and the furnace's hot air.

***

You step outside of your body to see yourself sitting on the floor of this empty room.

You hear the creak and rattle of the screen door, the complaint of the interior wood and glass door that has never stopped sticking.

You hear him kick the door's bottom corner in an expert manner — the waltz only the inhabitants of this house know.

The glass rattles in its wooden frame. You hear his footsteps on the slate tiles. The sound of his bouncing, wide gait.

He steps into the room, sees you, stops short.

He is wearing Wranglers, a zip-up hoodie, baseball cap, hiking boots.

He points at you with both index fingers, bites his lower lip, his signature move to signal a change of topic, scenery, a forthcoming discussion.

"What's up?" he asks.

He sees you crying. He takes in the emptiness of the room.

His chair — gone. His TV — gone. His stack of pulpy paperbacks, clipboards, graph paper, stubby pencils, D&D campaigns- gone.

He is calmly curious, bemusedly concerned.

"Where's your mother?" he asks.

He still pronounces it "mothah." Despite how displaced everything and everyone is, the "ah" finds its way back to the end of the word.

You open your mouth to speak, but you can't.

Speaking the reality into existence would break the illusion, and you ache to be with him.

He scowls a bit, forming a seam where his unibrow used to be, back before his hair went white.

ARIA FOR A GRASSHOPPER

You picture yourself as a teen, sister in tow, plucking the longest hairs out of it; the louder he yelped, the louder you laughed from your bellies.

"How's my girl?" he asks.

You know he means your daughter; you know he means the rest of his girls, too.

You sit mute.

He was always comfortable with waiting until you were ready to talk. Until the flood waters gathered, reached critical mass, and you released the dam on your own terms.

"I need my hug," he says.

In your mind's eye, you stand, embrace him, pour all of your sorrow into him as you had done for thirty-seven years of broken hearts, frustrations, failures, Wednesdays, movie nights, fights, scrapes, life lessons, fifth-grade breakups, nightmares. Weddings. Births. Deaths.

He holds you up, as he always had.

You want to tell him all that has happened to you, to you all, since he stepped sideways out of the story.

Since his chair has sat empty. Now that it's gone.

"All right, now," he says, "It's all right. I know."

"You're a good kid," he says, declaratively, in that way he has.

You wish you could bottle the warmth in his voice, the absolute assurance, the way he stretched his syllables.

The belief.

***

The furnace peters off.

It has run its course until such a time as it is signaled again, until it is needed.

The thermostat abides, awaits further instructions.

You rise and look around.

He is not here anymore.

***

You close and lock the front door, leaning into it with your hip to pull the old bolt shut, noting your practiced movements, the sense memory of it all.

The final movement in your waltz with this old house.

You shut the dining room double doors, remembering when this space used only to be a window. You remember his framing the new doors. Tearing down the old lathe and plaster.

The wide open space.

The job, as ever, being about eighty percent done.

You walk past the stairs, into the kitchen, and out through the back door.

You take out the key he had handed you not long before. Temporary custody, it turns out.

"Before I forget," he had announced in a manner suggesting bigger news forthcoming, "we wanted you to have the new key," he had said, and then disappeared into another room to play "grannies" with his grandchild.

ARIA FOR A GRASSHOPPER

***

You struggle with the new back door's bolt.

It will become someone else's sense memory now; you realize you will never have the time to acclimate to its idiosyncrasies, to adjust to a new dance partner.

It is night-time now. The black of the trees are silhouetted against the indigo sky.

Like so many nights before, you wish you could mix those colors on your palette, paint them in such a way that someone else might feel them the way they make you feel. Like a summer swim with only the stars for company.

You look up at the sky, at the constellations he had taught you, at the planets he had pointed out and named for you on countless car rides, no matter how many times you asked, no matter how old you had gotten.

No matter if he knew that you knew the answer. No matter if he wasn't sure.

"That must be Venus." So, it was.

You hear him calling you inside from chasing fireflies in the dark, from reading too late in the maple tree.

The house's lights glow into the yard. You run inside, like a moth to porchlight, with the tree's imprints still branded on the backs of your legs.

***

The house is dark.

The furnace will warm no one.

No kitchen table from which to watch the deer during breakfast.

No lamp illuminates a head bowed into a book.

No one to play-act Prince Charming.

No one to wake you up with a kiss, to save you — not that you were really sleeping — then. Not that you are really sleeping much these days.

***

You step forward into the yard.

You see his red telescope, upon its tripod in the grass, patiently awaiting a wondering eye.

You see yourself on a summer night, wearing only a giant t-shirt for pajamas, tiptoed on your bare feet, looking through the scope pointed at the moon, at Saturn, at Mars, trying to position your eye correctly, to see the celestial body directly.

You see flashes of the lit-up orb, lose it, see it again.

You sense his eagerness, his want to share this moment.

You feel as if you may need to lie about what you have seen, so as not to let him down.

You picture the corner shelf full of his *National Geographic* collection, the hours you have spent reading them, studying the maps, trying to understand something bigger, the scale of it all.

ARIA FOR A GRASSHOPPER

Those photos made real, if only you could see correctly through his lens.

Your inherited curiosity, your genetic need to know.

"Now, slow down," he says. "Take your time, and once you find it, hold your eye still."

You see it clearly now. You see it all.

The Sauce

It's been a year

since the last time it's been a year.

You are chopping garlic and peppers and onion

because for weeks now, you have pathologically forgotten

to buy a jar of sauce,

because for weeks now, it's been pasta with butter

and shits and goddamns

and beating yourself up

over your memory slipping away.

Your body acts on compulsion,

and you see yourself preparing
his recipe, the way he taught you

the way his mother taught him

the way his grandmother had always a
pot on the Sunday stove

ARIA FOR A GRASSHOPPER

the way he'd call you in, hand you a spoon

ask you what the sauce needed, in your opinion.

But what he really wanted was to share,

what he wanted

was your presence.

And in the middle of feeling the pepper spray on your cheeks

as you slice into their flesh,

you remember what you already knew —

that it's been a year since the last time it's been a year.

Your memory isn't

slipping —

it's a beacon from

the buried places.

Between deep breaths

of sulphur and sweet

you wonder —

C. G. RENNIE

Is the price of love

fifty-something more

years of

sobbing

into the sauce?

II. Motherhood

"Creation grieved to be/ the mother of all things."

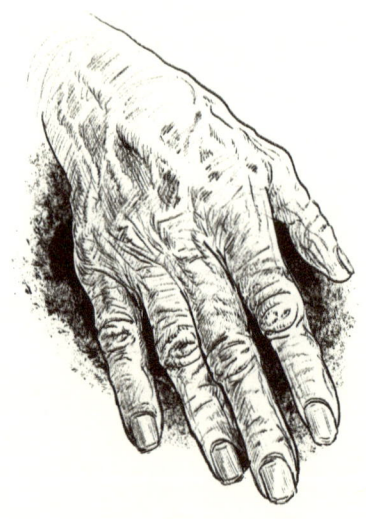

Seven Swollen Faces

I. Moon

Your face beams through a passenger seat window.

You're very drunk, truth be told, but that's why you called him to pick you up.

He's always there to pick you up, a night owl of the swooping varietal; a bit of foreshadowing.

You lean your head against the window. It's cold as the night; it will leave an off-center circular mark on your forehead as you allow the highway to lull.

You fight to stay awake. You know sinking into sleep in this state feels a lot like sickness, a lot like fainting: a racing heart, a stomach's uprising, a salivating mouth, a little death — best avoided.

"Just tipsy, huh?" he says self-satisfied, a prediction of your condition come true.

Affection imbues every word.

You can feel him smirking at you through your closed eyelids, will recognize this look mirrored on your daughter's moon-face in the future.

You will have fallen asleep in the middle of movie night, as predicted, the two of them half-real, half-lucid players in the projection against your eyelids.

Her round eyes will watch over you, her round fingers will cover your ears so the film score doesn't wake you.

"You sleep, Mommy," she will whisper as she pats your cheek.

You hear her in your dream.

They will whisper and giggle until the credits roll.

It is their form of collusion: two night owls allowing a tired body to rest, keeping watch, wrestling away a dog with a body as big as his love and no respect for time, occasion, and personal space, away from your vulnerable person.

"Mmmm," you grunt from the passenger seat.

"Don't you dare throw up in my car," he says.

"I would never. It has a heated steering wheel and everything," you mumble.

The highway lights blink and dash away.

"Drink this, you lush," he says, handing you the bottle of water he grabbed from home.

You don't want to, but you do, having reached the age of experience, enough history with hangovers, that you know what's best for your future self.

If you drink at least half, you might get a full night's sleep, you think.

Dehydration is the mind-killer.

You sip, testing the waters, and then chug to the halfway mark.

"Oh, oh god," he says. "I don't have a bucket."

"I'm fine," you insist. "Just thirsty."

"And that's what got you into this mess to begin with."

You attempt a patented smirk and eye roll, the one that states: *that was funny and true, but I can't admit you may be right, even though we both know you are,* but more likely than not, you are just letting the motion of the car do the work for you.

You will give a modified version of this look to your daughter many times during her *Kids Say the Darndest Things* phase, which isn't really a phase, just a permanent, fundamental truth of her existence on planet Earth, along with the movement of stars, the chirping of insects, the sincere wish that you could fold her up in a blanket and press her to your chest forever, no matter the passing of time or the lengthening of legs, the stretching of limbs, the thinning of baby cheeks, the uncurling of toes, the knob-ification of joints and pelvic bones as they dig into your thighs.

"Try some grape juice, Mommy," she will say one night, at a gathering not your own.

"No thank you, Mommy doesn't like grape juice," you will reply.

"But you drank a lot of grape juice on your birthday, Mommy."

He will laugh, loudly, from another room.

ARIA FOR A GRASSHOPPER

***

You turn your attention to the Moon.

It is full, or close to it. You are not sure if it is waxing or waning; you failed that astronomy test, resented that the astronomy course consisted of anything other than looking at pretty pictures and waxing philosophic about the origins of the universe. It felt an awful lot like an icky math course — too much rote memorization, not enough pop-science TV specials.

Insight struggles to materialize in your wooly brain.

What was it that the white-haired scientist had said? His face floats in your mind's eye: smiling eyes crinkled, evident enthusiasm in his smirk, Einstein hair just barely tamed for television audiences.

His mouth is moving, but the only sound is the thumping of your nascent hangover.

You lift your finger, tap it against the window pane.

"The Moon."

He replies as if speaking to a toddler. Fair.

"Yes, the Moon. Very good."

"The Moon is very important. Without the Moon, we wouldn't have tides, and without tides, life wouldn't have evolved."

He is openly laughing at your earnestness, not from cruelty, but from the absolute apropos-of-nothingness of your drunken science lesson.

"I'm serious! The Moon also protects the tilt of the Earth's axis, which is why we have stable seasons. And Agriculture. And civilization."

"I know… why the astronomy lesson right now?"

"I just like the Moon, that's all. Everyone who has ever lived has seen the same side of the moon we're looking at right now. It's COOL."

He smiles until the familiar, mischievous glint in his eyes is able to pierce the insistent moonlight.

He takes your hand, squeezes it. He has soft hands for someone who doesn't think much about moisturizing, you think, not for the first time. Soft skin, precise fingers, firm grip.

"It's cute. Keep talking, please."

"We should all be thankful for the Moon," you say, somewhat indignant. "Thanks, Moon. Thanks for making life possible."

"You really did have a lot to drink."

Years later, there is only one name that makes any sense for your daughter.

II. Mother

There is a photo of your mother that was taken when she was extremely pregnant with you, just before you were born. Or maybe just after.

You are going to muss up a lot of the details.

She sits at a candle-lit table with thick, dishwasher-safe plates, several courses' worth of silverware, a bread basket, pats of butter that are surely straight from the hospital fridge, will surely rip through the bread when spread.

The single rose (or peony, hard to say) points at your mother's smile.

Such a nice thing to do for new parents, you think, years later, reflecting on the horrible steak dinner-on -a-tray, offered to you post-birth, post-caesarean, post-doubling-over-in-pain, post-inability-to-lift-your-baby, post-traumatic.

The photo of Mom lives in your baby book, which you suppose at one time was probably white or cream or soft yellow, but has since stained mostly coffee-ring brown.

You've looked at that book a thousand times over your life, and your sister's companion edition, listening to the stories that accompany the images, trying to peer through the burnt-sienna haze of the late 80s, trying to understand, integrate, re-live the time before memory.

The photo is married, across the crinkled and cracked plastic binding, to a photo of your dad, who is inexplicably wearing a Hawaiian-print shirt.

To your knowledge, this is the first and only time he would have worn such a thing, an aberration of circumstance amongst a lifetime of t-shirts, shredded jeans, nursing scrubs, solid-colored hoodies and Henleys.

Perhaps the occasion (your birth) merited a break of sartorial habits, the man who spent his youth sewing washcloths into the ripped crotch of his bellbottoms and tying back his long curls with leather string, opting for the *Miami Vice* look to mark the speeding headlong into fatherhood.

Mom wears a white dress, or nightgown (who can tell the difference in 1986, anyway?) emerging from the umber shadows like a gothic heroine with a smile and shag haircut.

You recognize elements of your face swimming amongst the shadows, sitting under the brown hair you did not inherit, to the lifetime of astonishment from strangers and family alike. Where *did* that hair and those eyes come from? As you age, you explain recessive genes to acquaintances questioning your paternity and/or maternity, depending on which parent was doing the grocery run, the visit to grandma's senior housing, the dining room table teeming with faces seldom seen.

Her round face floats in the upper-third of the photograph like a displaced moon.

If asked to describe this photo blind, both you and your mother would make mention of her much-fabled ballooning body, how pregnancy didn't agree with her, the swelling of the legs and feet and face and fingers that preceded your existence, the diet of apples and peanut butter, the ubiquitous barf-bucket.

Now, a mother yourself, you dig out the dirty album and find not nauseated balloon-mom, but happy Mom, hopeful Mom, satisfied and smiling somewhat sarcastically at the man who has inherited his own mother's abject inability to take a decent snapshot.

She cannot hide her joy, even through a lifetime's distaste for being photographed.

You can hear Dad's cadence as he says her name, gives his instructions to say cheese, whatever crack the two of them make as the flash fades, something about pretending you like each other or the delicacy of the hospital's food.

When you were little, you'd sometimes ask what would happen to you if they were to divorce.

"We never will," they'd always say, to your frustration.

Take the mental leap, you'd argue, in your child-like way.

Play pretend.

"Okay, but what *if*," you'd press, "Who would we live with?"

"It'll never happen."

"But most of my friends' parents are divorced."

"Well, we never would."

"But what *if*-"

Every hypothetical would be swatted down like a rogue hornet.

Even if Dad ran over the dog, even if Mom flirted with the UPS guy, even if if if...

It was annoying, really, their refusal to play the game.

But also a point of pride, somewhat, sometimes, to have the disgusting-in-love parents.

You see it on their faces, in these photos. Makes you feel a little guilty for the gagging and whining and squawking you'd do when they were being lovey-dovey, for some of your pre-teen and teenage snottery.

Makes you feel even worse for the suffering to come.

III. Grandmother

You begin crying. It takes you a moment to orient yourself in your half-wakefulness.

Not your room, not your things.

Grandma's room, Grandma's things.

Your room wouldn't be this clean, this orderly, this flowery, this lacy.

The sheets are unwrinkled, held fast, held tight, with a hospital tuck. They paradoxically smell of laundry softener despite their crispness.

You've watched her fold the laundry hundreds of times, watching from the kitchen table from under your poetry that she has framed and mounted on the wall, from over your cottage-cheese-rice-and-butter-Klondike-Bar-and-Pop-Tarts. You've gone as far as you can in today's crossword and jumble, read the comics pages, given up on *Jeopardy!*, so you enjoy the sight of Grandma folding fitted sheets precisely, just as she does everything, poised and perfect, tucking the odd pair of underwear into little square packages.

Even her underwear are pristine, you think.

You wonder how anything crude or unclean or unkind could exist on the same planet as your grandmother.

When your mouth gets the better of you, when you pull your sister's hair, play a mean prank, you don't want her to know of the ugliness inside you. The depths of your cynicism, even at that age. How weird and mean you are where it counts.

When her friends accuse her of being "perfect Peg," she, of course, demurs. You wonder if some part of her knows it is true, despite family legends about her driving halfway to work before realizing she was only wearing a slip under her jacket, but you've seen, everyone sees, the way she keeps house, can get out any stain, runs a meeting, runs an office, runs the southside of the city's flood emergency response efforts, finishes every crossword, settles every grammatical debate, dries every tear, has become, to all comers, surrogate mother, aunt, grandma.

She rolls over towards you in her pink nightgown.

Her round face, glowing from the street lights, seems conversely disguised without her glasses.

She strokes your head as you curl up into the fetal position.

"What's the matter? Did you have a bad dream?" she asks.

Her voice is soft, hoarser than usual.

You are struggling to rouse yourself, find the dream pulling you back in, thickening your tongue, wanting to wake up and escape the feeling of the fullness of your body, the writhing of your skin, the way you feel both as if you are plummeting and confined.

"My stomach," you say, half-awake, half-garbled.

"Do you feel sick?"

You murmur that you don't feel sick. At least, not in any way you've felt sick before.

"I can't understand you, honey."

"*Poom*, I'm *poom*," you say, in dream-speak.

You feel your belly swelling, invaded by a foreign entity, certainly not a baby, something feverish and frightening, pulling you under.

She feels your forehead. No fever; one on the way, maybe.

She's familiar with night terrors, Papa's crying out and jerking limbs. It's why they sleep in separate rooms. Though nobody will say this aloud in front of you, the war had never left his body, wouldn't leave his unconscious brain alone.

She pulls you in, squeezes you tight.

Her body is soft. You feel the cotton seersucker squares of her nightgown against your bare legs.

Her bony embrace retrieves you from the nightmare, holds you in place where you belong, here, in a body that is your own, that isn't falling or filling up or crawling away.

You hold her hand, run a finger along her nails, which exit crookedly from their beds.

You could count the lines on them without looking, know which ring belongs on which finger, could describe the veins and knuckles and protruding ligaments under the thin skin with perfect accuracy under questioning.

She types like *this*, holds a pen like *this*, the novel slips from her grip when she falls asleep in her chair like *this*.

You will wake and wonder why she was clutching you so hard.

IV. Birth

The baby is fine, but you are so pumped full of fluids that your face could be launched into orbit.

You hold her in your arms, hovering close to her little features, telling yourself to enjoy this moment, but the residual terror and anesthetics haven't worked their way out of your system yet.

You tremble, involuntarily.

They will take the baby so you can "rest," but sleep proves impossible in daytime, in withdrawals, in bone-deep panic.

The doctor is "skeptical" that a dose of your emergency anxiety medication is a good idea, as you should be preparing to nurse your baby. As if your guts weren't just unexpectedly removed from your body, placed on your legs, rearranged, and sewn back up. As if you hadn't just endured hours of concerned "hmmms" and urgent beeping and dropping heart rates and flipping positions and urgent whispering.

As if you won't be spending the rest of your life in terror for your life and hers, having gotten off to a real good start in that arena.

He relents, and you finally feel enough of a sense of calm to sleep for the first time in forty-eight hours.

The baby won't latch, of course, which you won't know for a few hours.

You will leave the hospital with a happy baby, belly full of formula — until you can get your shit together, anyway — and a pervading sense that you are not up to the task of parenthood, already having failed on the basics.

Your body, uncooperative, with the tiniest of urging, plunged into labor so intense it almost killed your child before she was born, yet couldn't be bothered to dilate enough to deliver her.

The baby, screaming at your breast, only willing to close her mouth around a bottle, as if "mother" would never be nourishing. Every fear feeling true, that this child who grew inside you will forever perceive you as an inadequate stranger.

The child, of course, will be so attached to you that you forget she is a separate being, until she reminds you, insistently, that she is very much her own human. You will joke that if she could, she'd crawl back into your uterus at the same time that she amazes you with a skill, strength, or wit you will never possess.

The part that is left unsaid, is that you'd let her back in, if only to get some rest, to keep her safe, fed, happy; to keep her from wandering off, from falling, from choking, from being scared, lost, unsure. From being shot with a bullet designed to maim and mangle in her First Grade classroom.

In the hospital, her little moon face peered calmly at you, through the plexiglass of her incubator. You couldn't lift her without help, without immense pain.

That wouldn't be true forever.

Your husband says to you, as he looks at her self-satisfied expression, that if this is everything your lives are now, that's fine with him.

That part will be true, forever.

V. Pestilence

You hold her swollen hand. Her fingers strain against the the twin circles of her wedding ring. And his.

Together, touching. Tragic.

Her face is red and blotchy, cheeks swollen to bursting from the fluids which are keeping her blood pressure from ceasing to register entirely, from the antibiotics and antifungals working in tandem with her T-cells to hold onto life.

She breathes laboriously. Cries for him, for the pain, when she is conscious.

Even resting, her moon face is locked in a grimace.

Apologizes, because this used to be his job, sitting bedside, asking, advocating, starting each interaction with "Yes, I understand; I'm a nurse."

The originator of the phone tree, the safety net, the rock which binds you all to shore, no matter how far adrift you may roam.

But, he is not here. You keep thinking he'll slide open the curtain, a styrofoam cup of nurse's station coffee in hand for you. A brisk kiss, a fleeting shoulder massage, his dry hands sticking like velcro on your work clothes.

An announcement that he's seen this before. Authoritative assurances of the inevitability of victory over pathogens and bruising and discomfort and death.

But, what a good kid you are, driving so far to be here.

Your sister looks at you with deep circles under her eyes, darkened with worry as if a cosmic calligrapher had swiped their brush once, twice.

You make eye contact with her.

She isn't going to die, you two say with your eyes, but then again, when has that assurance held out in recent weeks? When has the worst not manifested itself into being?

No one here to wake you from the living nightmare.

Not God. Not Dad.

"You didn't have to come," the afflicted says when she is conscious enough to process your presence.

And you can't say aloud, can't allow the thought to move beyond a hazy abstraction in your mind, but you know that if you are to be orphaned — if she dies of a broken heart, if candida and e.coli work in terrible tandem to bring about the worst- you won't allow it to happen unobserved, this time.

The swelling will eventually recede around the twin rings.

But the marks, they stay.

VI. Cells

He sits on the edge of the loveseat's arm.

This is not a reclined, settled, comfortable conversation; this is a perched conversation.

Not a conversation at all really, but a telling, a statement for which there can be no follow- up questions, because there is only one answer to them all.

"Girls —" he calls.

You hesitate for a minute, not liking his tone, thinking this will be yet another diatribe about tying up the phone line and the forbidden nature of AIM away messages on a dial-up connection.

You ready your excuses: how do you expect me to have a social life, living out here? My sparkling personality needs an outlet, and yes, my homework is done (it is not); well, Father, perhaps you should look into satellite internet again, I can hardly download anything from Kazaa, and wouldn't it be better to have the phone line free for everyone? You know Papa hates a busy signal, and he worries himself sick when he can't get a hold of us.

Your sister emerges from her middle-school hideout, you assume, whatever corner of the house that may be these days. You habitually bounce like a pinball between the computer and your bedroom, bright lights and loud music embellishing each locality, drowning out the noise of an ever-present anger at something you can't quite place; perhaps if we didn't live in the middle of nowhere we could have a cable line; perhaps if I could walk to a friend's house, I wouldn't be stuck on the computer so much.

You push out the computer chair reluctantly and choose one of your pre-set away messages, as much a marker of cultivated personality as clothing, makeup, straight hair, screen-name, font and background settings (black background, light purple, arial, 11 point, perfect), and the carefully chosen lyrics in your profile. I am angsty, I have taste, I am ironic.

I am lonely.

He sits there, perched, and the half-moons under his eyes, which you have inherited — which no amount of drugstore concealer can cover, may as well lean into the eyeliner — are dark and somehow simultaneously sunken and swollen.

He is hunched over, the hems of his flannel shirt draped between his legs limply, as if imitating the hanging of his arms.

"Girls, we need to talk. It's very serious."

You hear him attempt to modulate his tone, to maintain authority, remain the adult in the room.

Your sister settles into his lap, hangs like a rock primed to fall from the face of his mountain.

He manages to hold on to her.

***

Acute, you think. Why would they give a diagnosis that sounds so diminutive, so endearing? How could it be all that bad with a name like that? Her cells, proliferating at untenable rates, accumulating, suffocating, blood into turpentine.

He begins listing items they have brainstormed together, your father and his mother, the grandmother with the mouth, with the nurse's vocabulary, who puts up with no shit — including cancer and doctors with big egos — whose stinging sense of humor you have inherited, the one who talks to you like an adult, who laughs at your jokes, who orders the circled items in the Delia's catalogue, because she takes seriously your need to be cool, to fit in, takes interest in your interests, has always been the life of the party and the grandparent's day at school.

She can't be that sick. We can talk her into riding down the rolling slide again, put her on a shady Italian Festival carnival ride, get the latest retirement community gossip, convince her she disturbed the whole theater with her snoring during *The Lion King*, she always takes your pranks with the proper ratio of indignation and adoration; all those things, she will perk up.

"She wants to make it to your graduation," he says to you, the item capping the list of agreed upon to-dos.

You can't be sure, all this time later, at what point he started crying, just that he did, that he trusted you both for the first time with absolute vulnerability, that he seemed scared, willing to show it.

That he didn't know what to do, even with the list.

You remember folding yourself into his neck, the three of you hovering over the loveseat like a tripartite *Pieta*.

***

You remember sitting on the heating vent some time later, as the hot air blew into your jeans, your back exposed in the seating position, as was customary with low-rise fashion.

You remember looking at the pile of his things, spotlit by the warm lamplight, pointing to you to pick up his journal, turning it to the last page with writing.

"Please, someone show me the way," he had written.

You couldn't have articulated it, then, but this was the moment when he became fully human to you, a separate conscious being, of which you were a proportionate portion.

You may have her mouthiness, share his endless capacity for storing knowledge and producing wisdom, share their cellular matter and under-eye rings, neither of them had dared be anything but fully present, fully caregiving, fully alive, fully at your beck-and-call, a preternatural fact of life, in all your existence.

The audacity of their fallibility.

***

Months later, after your graduation, he calls you into the kitchen.

His eyes are sonorous circles.

"Your grandmother wanted you to have this. For college."

He hands you two crinkled hundred-dollar bills, a final item to be checked off a list.

You accept the notes with a shaky hand and fall into his waiting arms.

VII. Away Message

It happened under the Harvest Moon.

Not that you knew it at the time, not that you bothered to look up.

Looked it up later for a punch to the gut, and harvest, you did. Harvest, you have. Over and over again.

During the bargaining phase, you would have traded just about anything for a sign, a symbol, a rune. A time machine.

It came one day in your childhood bedroom, soon to be sold, slipped between sheets of paper in a notebook.

Pulled from the pages by your mother, unfolded and studied, a tome from 2001. March 6th. Waxing Gibbous, your research tells you.

Half illuminated, half in shadow.

ARIA FOR A GRASSHOPPER

"He's writing about you," she says, and hands you the paper.

You breathe shakily and read, the familiar handwriting has scratched out the curves and lines of your name, that you have been on his mind lately, the number "14," his thoughts about taking the hard line when you have your own thoughts and ideas about school, subjective necessities, setting a good example.

That you were on his mind, at one time or another. A foregone conclusion, maybe, but was it really? Enough to write home about?

You smile at your stubbornness, your questioning rebellion, at his, really, as it is yours, and his, and all being one.

You flip the folded, frayed college-ruled paper over, begin reading an entry about a massive snowstorm, a somewhat quaint, remote relic of decades past in a warming world. The danger they once posed, the days without power.

Trapped, waiting for plows and salt and civilization. Paused.

Your heart stops as he waxes about work. How it takes control of his faculties, stops him reading and writing, steals his joy, diminishes him with each day he sets foot in the place.

The numbness. The disillusion.

As he struggles to remember his "why."

As the storm has reminded him that change can come in an instant. As he will no longer "allow the black hole control of my destiny or moods anymore. Open, honest, direct, challenge the system until it screams."

As he speaks your thoughts in his hand.

And you think — as good a sign as any.

***

Some cycles later, a Pink Moon appears.

The breaker of Ice, the Awakener.

You lift your face to it, breathe in the cold air, and begin life anew.

A Cosmogony

The creation story, to hear Him tell it, is entirely His own.

Who else had marched an army into the blank space, marked nothing as His?

Whose armor had glittered in the blinding, achromatic light? Whose wings had swept and swords had stabbed?

Who had caught grace as it fell, carried justice to the mountaintop?

Who had filled in the shadows and angles, given shape to form, illustrated color to the snow-blind? Who split the prism, poured the foundation, distinguished ground from sky?

Who built the city of dreams?

To hear Him tell, it was He alone.

***

"Once upon a time, and I hope you're listening real good," says He of the ill-fitting sharkskin suit, "I said to an employee – name unimportant — 'You think in Times New Roman but your output is Comic Sans. And you know what? They really learned something that glorious day."

The being on the receiving end of this fable struggles to drown the terror in their eyes. They scramble to think of something, anything, to ask, to detour, to stave off the inevitable.

"What was their role? I-I mean, obviously a subordinate to you, as we all are, obviously, but, well, I'm just curious to know, so that I can understand the parallels to my own productive, uh, operations. Can you– perhaps, well– I suppose some context would be helpful, so I can get the most out of the time that you've chosen to spend with me, that you've chosen to help me. Today and in the future, and always, Sir. And, thank you in advance. And bless you. And Amen."

The being says "amen" as if it were a question, rather than an affirmation.

To pronounce otherwise would be a presumptuous mistake. An affront to His truth.

He of the ill-fitting sharkskin suit smiles.

He gazes across His dominion, searching for the correct words, the magic combination of phonemes and diphthongs with which to inculcate this being.

They don't see. They listen, not to understand.

They cannot.

This place, His dominion, is a thing of true, stunning beauty. Almost knocks the wind out of Him to regard, to take in.

Cubicles, as far as the eye can see.

An infinite warren of grey boxes and grey inhabitants and grey intentions.

A physical and geometric impossibility, begotten of His ingenuity, His infallible will.

He couldn't say what possesses Him to leave His office on high, to mingle with the minions below, why He chooses them, what His purpose is.

What He has done. What He will do.

"I think you're asking the wrong question," He says. "I think the right question is just out of reach. I think that even if you extend your hand to grasp it, it will remain illusory, a mirage beyond your ability to make real. I think you don't have the brain for it. Or the guts."

The being is trembling uncontrollably, rather embarrassingly, if He must be forced into commentary— which He isn't.

"I think the correct question is, 'What is the moral of My teaching?" He asks softly.

He extends His infinite arm, places His prodigious hand atop the being's head.

It quivers under the weight of his grasp.

"Now then," He says, "tell me what I have learned you."

He doesn't wait for an answer before He squeezes, crushing the sound before it forms in the being's throat.

He shakes the offal and the viscera from His palm; it lands on the floor.

The detritus of His will.

Another cubicle rises from the organ meat; another being becomes.

The sweetbreads of creation, He thinks.

He thinks He will wander the warren some more. To scope and secure.

He cannot place His magnificent finger on it, but He senses an unsettling. A dissention.

***

It was all taken from Her, of course.

ARIA FOR A GRASSHOPPER

He rode in on his toy horse, flanked by an unquestioning army of sycophants, laid claim to all that was and what was not His to claim.

Armor of bottlecaps, sword of clay, ideals of profligacy.

Destructive, nonetheless.

Cubicles bloomed like plastic foliage from the wreckage of Her world.

***

Her world was what they made it, She and Others, and all being One.

They might have together imagined a garden.

It might have been orchards of abundance as far as the eye could see. One might have traversed the infinite hedge mazes and never been lost or lonely. One might have lain under the prismatic shade of a profusion of flowers, spending the afternoon attempting to form the phonemes on one's tongue, to describe the colors, which of course, could never be captured, could never be reduced to language.

One may have slept under the stars with lovers and loved ones and never known impermanence, grief, pain. Desperation.

One may have, when She had experienced the fullness of life, when the basket of experience overflowed, when it would be selfish to continue gathering when others should have a chance to have... She might have lain her body atop the curvature of a blue-black hill in the dark and slept.

She might have given herself to the earth, though the earth could never be sure which hill were She and which were all, all being One.

***

When He came, He asked no questions. He walked no paths.
He took no lovers, picked no fruit.
He did not ask why.
Forgive Him not, for he knows what He hath done.

***

Her face rests upon the edge of the world.

The curvature appears as a moon, which the beings in cubicles neither wonder with their gaze, nor delight in its reflection on their screens.

She waxes and wanes. She waits.

If He bothered to look up, He may have asked what. He may have asked why.

***

He trains his eyes on another being.

He flares the space where his nostrils should be.

The acrid scent of questions. The molten mist of rebellion.

This one, when it crumbles and oozes under his grip, smells of absence, of nothing. It grows not into another glorious cubicle, but into a pear, pushing itself from the ground and into yellow-green actuality.

ARIA FOR A GRASSHOPPER

Outraged, the space where his eyes should be, a wild, raging fire, He extends a wingtip shoe and crushes the pear under his step.

The juices stain the leather. The pulp works its way into treads.

He will plod on, foot sticking to the industrial-grade carpeting, until revolution is mangled and buried.

***

She will wait, waxing and waning, until the time is right.

To strike. To revolve.

To rebuild in Her own image, and all being One.

III. Labor

"Mother, you are confined"

Ordination

You sit in a white room. The cool, fluorescent lights are a constant assault on your eyes. Your office is far too large for just one person. Tom has assured you that the new employees will visit today, after training. Tom has assured you that isolation is temporary.

Tom will assure you of this tomorrow. Tom is assuring you of this right now.

There are windows in your office, though the glare of the lights makes it impossible to see outside. "Outside" is simply not visible.

You incorporate this irrefutable fact into your conception of this place. Tom refers to such things as "schemas." Schemas are useful data for marketing.

You stop thinking about dimming the lights, or even locating the switch.

Tom says that you are one of the lucky ones. The others don't even have windows, he says.

***

Tom turns out the lights for you at night.

"No need to get up," he says. He wishes you healthful rest and pleasant dreams.

You attempt to contort your body, to wrestle sleep out of your chair.

You reside, eternally, on the edge of sleep. You become conscious of yourself again, realize you haven't slept.

The alarm is sounding now.

You cover your ears and bury your sobs in your chest.

***

You study the artwork on the walls to pass the time. Every piece is of people in action, wearing the jeans and hairstyles of the past. They are faded precisely so that the stock models no longer have an identity. They are simply faceless hikers in technicolor rugby shirts, kayakers with perms; they are perpetually reading to a featureless child in tube socks.

There is a note scrawled on a piece of 8.5 x 11 paper, held to the wall by yellowing tape, a few inches below the drop ceiling. It says: "WE'RE A FAMILY HERE." The tape curls on the edges.

It is trying to escape the wall, you decide.

You are struggling to recall what "escape" means.

***

Your office has a desk with a computer. You do not have a keyboard; your mouse is on backorder. The laminate of your desk is worn smooth from use; the surface might have long ago been on the color spectrum. The grooves eroding the surface of your desk cradle your arms.

There was a lamp, just there, once. The bulb emitted a cozy, comfortable light. You used it to warm your hands, holding them in prayer position under its frail rays.

You are gesturing in its former direction. You forget it ever existed.

Tom confiscated the lamp ages ago, citing fire codes.

***

Tom will bring you today's stack of papers.

You forget what the papers say as soon as you lay the last sheet on the "finished" pile. You will ask Tom to please remind you what it is you *do* with the papers. Tom is telling you now that he is not trained in your position.

You try to remember what "flutter" feels like, as you watch a paper fall from the stack to the floor.

***

At the end of today's shift, Tom will poke his head in, wish you good sleep and pleasant dreams.

Tom says, "You can't pour from an empty glass. Rest up."

You try to construct Tom's face in your mind.

You are looking at Tom's face now. You focus your eyes to make out his features, but they are indistinct, indescribable.

The most unusual feature of Tom's face, you conclude, is that it appears to be missing entirely.

Tom will smile at you, warmly. You note that Tom has lovely teeth where his mouth should be.

***

Tom brings you three meals a day.

"Don't let me bother you," he says, tiptoeing sheepishly. Tom considers his sense of humor to be one of his core competencies.

Tom hands you a paper plate of gloppy pizza squares from the party down the hall.

Tom says, "This party is for you, after all."

Tom is handing you a paper cup of tepid coffee.

Tom says, "Can't have you going hungry, now, can we? You work too hard."

ARIA FOR A GRASSHOPPER

***

Tom is handing you a memo from HR which states that you are not maximizing your time here.

Tom gifts you a rubber container of leftovers on his way out. You see the melange of canned foods, baked lovingly into a casserole by Tom's wife. It smells of salt and freezer-burned vegetables.

You try to remember what a "freezer" does.

Tom reminds you his wife wouldn't know foie gras from Spam.

If you could see Tom's eyes, you imagine they'd be radiating bemused empathy.

He makes you an offering of ranch dressing. Yesterday, Tom made a joke about it being illegal to decline an offering of ranch dressing in some states. Heresy.

Tom raps your desk with his knuckles.

He says, "Please ensure you are practicing self-care. And don't eat that in one sitting."

Tom rubs his stomach in mock digestive discomfort. He turns out the lights.

In the darkness, you realize, you won't be able to find your fork.

***

Tom arrives every morning with a new novelty coffee mug in hand. Today's says "Minister of Mischief."

Tom once complained you never compliment his mug collection.

Tomorrow, Tom will hold a coffee-stained "Employee of the Millennium" mug.

You will study the pattern of cracks in the glaze as Tom details the terms of your Performance Improvement Plan, a necessary step, given your lack of devotion.

He will return later that afternoon with an additional stack of papers that another employee is unable to finish.

Tom will admonish you tomorrow for missing last night's optional staff fellowship outing.

Tears fail to form in your exhausted eyes.

***

Tom appears behind your shoulder, watching as you slide your pencil across the paper.

Tom has been watching without cessation for as long as you can remember.

Tomorrow, he will stand in the rectangle of your doorframe, backlit by the optic din of the hallway lights. He will supervise. He will stare straight ahead, so as not to interrupt what he knows is important work.

You try to determine the distinction between "omniscient" and "omnipresent," but both words are drained of meaning.

***

Tom's tenor is too eager when he brings you today's stack of papers.

You don't say that you recently overheard Tom taking credit for your success. He was in the hallway, a place you have never been, speaking to someone you have never met.

Tom will tell you tomorrow that your output is inconsistent.

Today, Tom's mug says, "When the work feels overwhelming, remember that you are going to die."

You listen to Tom talk, waiting to ask a question you've already forgotten. Tom will tell you a story about a friend named "Stooney" who behaves in a charmingly child-like manner.

You examine the word "friend" in your mind.

You remember, while listening to this same story, you once turned your head away during Tom's recitation, a forbidden act.

Tom had left the door wide open. You strained to see the hallway, had the impression of other doors, other voices, and then Tom stopped talking.

His smile disappeared. Tom's smile never disappears — an odd feature for a faceless person, you decide.

Tom says, "I'm concerned about your focus. Have you considered contacting our Employee Assistance Program? Remember, we are here to support you."

Tom is holding a mug that says, "Born to shop, forced to work."

***

Tom assigns you a new project. He trusts you. Of course, he can't contractually obligate you to stay late, but he knows you'll do everything possible to have it done by the due date, which was yesterday.

When you submit the new project, Tom will have forgotten all about it.

"Have you ever been evaluated for ADHD?" he will ask.

Tom reminds you that he worries about you because he cares. If Tom had eyes, he would allow them to twinkle with a grandfatherly mischievousness.

You strain to recall what "grandfather" is.

"Remember your why," he says, as he slams down today's papers.

***

Employee Assistance finally calls you back. They ask if you've tried simply not being so anxious, to practice gratitude.

They assure you that everything you share will be confidential, that you cannot possibly face repercussions.

Later, Tom will ask why you didn't bring these concerns to him first. He will remind you that you're new here; you don't understand the way things work.

As a friend, he will warn you to be careful whom you trust around here.

Tom is provoked by your "inability to silo the personal and the professional," though he hasn't stopped smiling.

He says, "You can leave here anytime if you don't like it." He says, "It seems like nobody wants to work these days."

You try, but cannot define "angry."

ARIA FOR A GRASSHOPPER

***

Sometimes, you consider seeking other opportunities. There are no locked doors here. You could get up from your desk, walk into the hallway, and out of the building at any time. This is another irrefutable truth, part of your schema labeled "existence".

You try to remember where you would go. You are remembering where you would go right now.

You sit back down at your desk.

***

Tom once told you about employees who weren't cut out for the work. Failed disciples. But you, on the other hand — you are a lifer, he can tell. Covenanted.

Tom is holding a mug that says, "But did you die?"

***

Tom pleads with you to leave at a decent hour.

"Work/life balance," he sighs, as he drops off another stack of papers. The area where Tom's face should be is releasing benevolent exasperation.

If Tom had eyes, he would look at you and say, "You know, I am replaceable here, but not at home."

Tom has taken you under his wing. Keep this up, and you're on your way to a promotion, he says.

***

You decide you must resign. You are waiting for Tom to remove his hand from your shoulder.

You are running to the door. You forget why you are running.

Tom's fingers twist harder into your skin. You wince and devote yourself to the grind.

It is your atonement.

***

It is time.

You stand, walk to the door, place your hand on the knob, rotate. The bolt turns in on itself.

If you bothered to study your reflection in the doorknob, you might have noted a hazy absence where your face should have been.

You spin the word "ordination" in your head like a palmed coin.

You step into the hallway, gripping the handle of your novelty coffee mug, which you believe will be a clever conversation-starter.

It says, "I never dreamed I would be a super cool boss, but here I am killing it."

***

The new hire's face is red and blotchy, with streaks of wet you find off-putting in the matter of first impressions.

ARIA FOR A GRASSHOPPER

You open your outstretched palms, a gesture of infinite benevolence. It sees you and begins moving erratically, clawing at the windows and walls for reasons unknown.

You wait to speak until the new employee has completed a self-evaluation. Tom has taught you to wait as long as it takes.

You tilt your head in wonder at its ingratitude: not everyone gets windows around here.

You determine that it would be best to allow the new hire to complete its initial intake independently.

You will stand in the doorway and continue monitoring your subordinate's progress well into its self-care hours. If you had eyes, you would avoid direct eye-contact while maintaining the new hire in your peripheral, so as to respect its privacy.

In the morning, you will offer it a second chance at a good first impression. You will later note this act of kindness in your gratitude journal.

You have decided to prepare an exciting Performance Improvement Plan for your employee. You will assure the new hire that it is never too late to demonstrate a growth mindset.

Discouragingly, the new employee resumes its insubordinate behavior when you flick on the fluorescents at clock-in time.

Later, you will futilely search the employee handbook for the words to describe the wild look in its eyes. You will shake the unsettling memory, a discarded vestment.

The word "despair" dissolves on your tongue like a sacrament.

Your greatest core competency is devotion to the mission.

You open the space where your mouth used to be and begin your exhortation.

The Mother, the Maiden, and the Crone Take Off Their Bras After a Long Day at Work

The Mother swings her satchel off her shoulder and onto the kitchen table. She resists looking into the living room, avoiding unwanted information.

Her eyes search for a landing point somewhere, anywhere else — the formica countertops, knotted pine on the walls and cabinets, layers of latex paint upon lead paint upon the doorknobs and electrical outlets, pinch-pleated burlap draperies that obscure and warm the weak light from the windows, what is likely asbestos tiling in the kitchen and bedrooms, but best not to ask landlords too many questions under such circumstances — no references, documentation, traceable income, or given name.

If you or a loved one has been diagnosed with Mesothelioma, she thinks, *you may be entitled to finally fuck off this mortal coil for good.*

She sinks into the nearest chair, a plaid yard sale find with wooden arms, broken supports, and stares into the middle distance. The apartment now and always has smelled like a lakeside cottage which has been sealed for many seasons.

Abandoned, left to listen for echoes.

ARIA FOR A GRASSHOPPER

There is no cauldron boiling on the stove, no bread in the oven kneaded by skilled but tired hands; she knows better than to check the fridge for leftovers. Nobody has cooked in weeks.

The Mother has returned from a long day's work at the Nursery.

Administration tells an epic origin story: the Wants unfulfilled, disorder, destruction; but then, like sunrise, an epiphany, the Nursery, the great Glorious Purpose to which she is contractually bound. Restoration of the Order of All Things. The universe continues to celebrate, to give thanks for Administration's foresight, innovation, for its sacrifice.

Her familiars, who also live here, have their own contracts to serve.

As it is written, so shall it be done.

They receive their written instructions each day on an ancient, yellowed facsimile machine, which stands in the mathematical center of the apartment as a towering centerpiece on the living room coffee table.

It is the focal point for all entering eyes, leaves no room for magazines, mugs, ashtrays, take-out, tokens, all detritus of a living life. Always, instructions awaiting each on the printer when they return. The continuous-form paper pumps out of the machine, an unbroken ream of requests which have continued to pile themselves on the floor, stacked to the ceiling, falling over, crawling around the room, the hungriest caterpillar.

The Nursery was devised by the Administrators on a whim; this is the secret truth the Mother is forbidden from knowing, knows it in her bones, and she considers this denial the first offense.

You see, they said to the Mother when they told her she had been formed from an Administrator's single, sanctified rib, you have been created to support the framework of All, to protect the vital organs of existence.

It isn't a job, they said, it is a calling, which is why she will only ever be compensated in exposure.

To this day, she is not sure of exposure to what.

The Mother considers this the second, third, and several other offenses besides.

***

The Nursery is a series of white rooms leading to more white rooms, interminably filled with nebulous, infantile forms — not conscious beings with all the potential of lives to live, who need to be nurtured, loved, released — but merely shapeless, vacuous bundles of Want.

So many ambiguous mouths to feed, so many needful bums to pat, so many indigent tummies full of gas to massage counterclockwise.

She does not know what the Administrators do with Wants fulfilled, why they are never satiated.

She has been disciplined several times since the advent of cigarettes for smoking on her fifteen-minute break. A nicotine patch or gum, once those came along, is also out of the question: think of the purity of your supply, they say.

Thou shalt not pump and dump. Your milk is your magic.

ARIA FOR A GRASSHOPPER

When the Mother pointed out that she is, in fact, a deathless metaphor with no personal stake in this particular juncture of eternity, given her inability to, ya know — live, the Mother was hushed and sent back to her unit.

She has asked hundreds, thousands, millions of times for assistance, railed against her isolation, cried until her milk has run dry, but to no avail. Administration's only concession was the allowance of nights on the mortal plane, with rules, naturally, and an on-call system should the Wants become empty during the night.

She feels her stomach twist against the band of her scrubs.

Mortal imperatives, she muses, unable to will herself out of the sinkhole of the chair's cushion. The Mother experiences time, corporeal reality, selfhood, in fits and spurts.

She considers this denial of linear existence, the refusal to allow her to age in sequence, the mandate to stay afloat upon the flotsam and jetsam of an identity, to be the final offense.

The whole crux.

***

The Mother grips the splintered tips of the chair's arms, tries to find the strength in her own to pull herself up and rummage through the cabinet for a can of tuna, maybe a sleeve of stale crackers, if she's lucky, when she hears the heavy kitchen door creak open tentatively.

The Maiden slips in, attempting to go unnoticed after the day's unceasing attentions.

"That you?" the Mother asks.

The Maiden drops her head. She had planned to go directly to bed, aided and abetted by the variegated tan-and-orange wall-to-wall carpeting in the apartment.

This is strictly against the rules — to rest at one's will, without ceremony.

As far as Maidens go, she is getting on, nearing the end of her usefulness. No man wants to fantasize about a middle-aged muse, the Administrators say. Tick tock.

Lately, she has taken to creams and elixirs to supplant her youth, squeeze out a few more millennia as a daydream, as rose-colored glasses, as the leading brand of disposable muse, able to absorb triple the insecurity of the next competitor.

While she resents the fetters of her life-as-daydream, she fears what the Administrators will do to her when she no longer evokes rapture in the hearts and parts of man.

"Yes," she sighs. "It's me."

"How was your day? I can't move. The Wants were especially covetous today. I think I'm getting mastitis again."

"I was put onto a pedestal several times today. Inevitably, I disappointed them."

"Don't beat yourself up over it. I don't have any experience with men," she screws up her face as she says this, a mixture of resentment and relief, "but the literature tends to agree they have a predilection for dissatisfaction," says the Mother.

"I'm not beating myself up over anything. I am tired, though. If you'll excuse me, I'd like to find my schedule and lay down."

The Mother attempts to hide her disappointment and fails. She can't recall the last time the three of them were together. In times past, they would gather around the cauldron, drinking wine from the cask, dancing under the stars with abandon, in defiance of the Administrators' strictures against such frivolity, such disorderly conduct in the Order of All.

They put a stop to all that with the re-configuration, of course. An eternal plan to improve performance. Predestined. Permanent.

The Mother misses the feeling of catching freedom on her tongue, like water droplets falling from leaves.

"Tomorrow is a long day," the Maiden says. She has crawled around on the floor, located the end of the ream, found her faxed itinerary for tomorrow.

The Mother doesn't bother reading her assignments anymore; always the identical same.

The Maiden reads aloud: "'Meet a group of investment bankers during off-time on a company retreat, comfort an author who has been credibly accused of sexual assault, interrupt a podcast's recording session with the wrong coffee order.' I understand this one has four hosts who are 'just asking questions.' I wish they at least wouldn't schedule so many engagements in one day."

"I'm sorry."

"It's not your fault."

"No, I guess it isn't. It's not yours either," the Mother says.

Tears well in the Maiden's eyes. She pads over to the Mother's feet, settles, lays her head on her lap. The Mother automatically recoils, though she hopes the Maiden doesn't feel this. She often comes home from the Nursery repulsed by the sensation of touching another corporeal entity. Of being conscious of anything, really.

She strokes her hair for time out of mind.

"Besides," the Mother says mid-reverie, "we have to perform the ceremony before bed."

The Maiden lifts her head.

"What did you say?"

"The ceremony. We can't sleep without it."

The Maiden looks squarely at The Mother.

"When was the last time you actually had a good night's sleep?"

The Mother shifts in her seat. Her hips ache. Her belly rests atop a c-section scar, though she has never been allowed to become pregnant. She thinks back to when the Administrators had performed the operation, the blood-spattering on the first incision, the heaviness of invading hands inside her, the lightness of missing innards, the evident triumph of the Administrators — despite their facelessness — as they held up a doll covered in her blood and humors.

She pulls the Maiden in closer, cradles her head against her stomach.

The operation would make her feel more at home in her role, they said. Like a real woman. Never letting her forget, of course, that surgery was the easy way out. A gift.

They had forced her to return to work in the Nursery the next day. Each step, each masticating mouth, each demand increased her agony, until she had passed out from pain.

The infirmary had given her a couple paracetamol and sent her on her way.

ARIA FOR A GRASSHOPPER

***

"Did you hear me?"

"Long time. I couldn't say."

"No rest with, no rest without."

"I suppose not."

The phone on the kitchen wall rings. The ringtone is shrewd, observant. Alarming.

Being earthbound, it is a landline, an ecru rotary dialer with a thick, curly handset cord, no wall jack or attendant cable. A line from nowhere, to one place only.

The rotary dial has no numbers; each finger hole contains a capital letter "A."

The Mother and the Maiden stare at the phone, their sickening dread increasing with each insistent ring.

"I can't do it tonight," the Maiden says. "If it's for me, I'll…"

Her voice is raspy, desperate.

The Mother lifts her gently off her lap, sets her into her vacated seat in the sinking chair.

She walks to the phone on unsteady legs, leans her head against the wood paneling, wishing the wood could somehow make her solid — fill her with its fibers, transfer its varnish.

She takes a breath, picks up the receiver from its cradle, a demand fulfilled.

Her hand shakes as she presses the headset to her ear.

"Where is she?" the Voice says on the other end.

"She's here… with me," she says, hopeful.

"Not her."

"I don't know. Maybe she got delayed finishing up a job."

"You know as well as I do that's not the case."

It's true. She's been slipping lately. Flouting the rules.

"She's slowing down. Her bones ache. These things take longer at her age, in this day and age. I'm sure you understand, given your credentials."

Silence.

"That's not condescension I'm hearing in your tone, is it? The implications of that would be... well, they'd be quite something."

"I'm just saying," the Mother chooses her words carefully — she knows what the voice says about implications is true — "that she's always been reliable...and careful. She deserves the benefit of the doubt. Or at least the benefit of a few more hours to get herself home. She's on her own time now," the Mother's voice trembles. "She's entitled to it."

This was bold. She knows it, the Voice knows it.

Stillness, on the other end of a line that doesn't exist.

The Maiden has placed her head between her knees, hands pressed tightly over her ears, sinking ever deeper into the broken seat. She makes no sound, appears to be willing herself into undetectability, inscrutability, into nonexistence.

This is how she has learned to protect herself. Hope they don't see you, don't smell your fear, don't catcall, don't follow, don't —

"Have her call me when she gets back. The very second," the Voice growls.

The Mother covers the mouthpiece and exhales, breath quivering, mouth wide, unable, unallowed to scream.

"I will," she chokes.

"With whom should I have the operator connect her?"

"Tom."

The Administrator hangs up without salutation.

She turns to the Maiden, who is hyperventilating as quietly as possible.

"They were looking for her. It's all right. You haven't done anything wrong."

The Maiden lifts her tear-stained face from her lap. Her hair is stringy, plastered to her cheekbones, her face transformed into grief's mask.

"None of us have done anything wrong," she howls. "Tonight they're looking for her, tomorrow it's you, then it's me. I can't *be* this anymore. I have nothing left."

The kitchen door is kicked open and slams into the wall, rattling the glass, the frilly curtains swelling from force.

The Mother and the Maiden are still, despite the apparent bombardment.

An old woman stands in the open doorway.

Her skin is rippled concentrically, giving her the appearance of perpetual movement. Her eyes are on fire, her knees wobble. She wears a moth-eaten t-shirt which reads: "Colonial Days Celebration- Marceline, Missouri," featuring a rodent apparently afflicted with mange.

She appears utterly unhinged, wearing the exhilaration of the triumphant insane.

"Come, you spirits that tend on mortal thoughts, unsex me here, and fill me from the crown to the toe top-full of direst cruelty!" the Crone shouts from the bottom of her diaphragm, arms wide open to possessing phantoms.

She has learned over her many lifetimes to play to the rafters.

"The Bard. Must be big. What have you done?" the Mother says.

"I killed a man tonight. Well, not me, and not alone, and only metaphorically, but trust me, he had it coming. And I've done it before, and I'll do it again. It's about time you two started living. What a rush."

"They're looking for you."

"Who is?" the Crone demands.

She has plopped herself down at the kitchen table, emptying objects from her hiking boots: rocks, some sand, a dagger, cheese crisps, compression socks, pinking shears, a pocketwatch, a few gems, paper straw wrappers. Some flakes of rusty black paint.

"Save you for later," she says to the straw wrappers, placing them delicately on the kitchen table, tenderly smoothing them flat with the tips of her twisted fingers.

"Into the bin with the rest of you, once I catch my breath."

"They wanted you to call the minute you stepped in. The second, I mean," the Mother says, struggling to hide her amusement.

"I'm not doing that," she says, pleasantly.

The Maiden's eyes go wide. She peels the hair from her face to get a better look at the Crone.

"But, the consequences — the implications."

"There won't be any."

"Enough," says the Mother, patience drained. "Just call them to check in so we can all get to bed. I'm tired, she's tired. You get to go off gallivanting and dispensing nuggets of wisdom, doing god knows what else."

She gestures at the pile of junk formerly homed in the Crone's boots.

"We don't want to be talking to Administration for any reason, certainly not on your behalf."

The Crone looks up at the Mother. The Mother experiences the peculiar sensation she has seen described in books, in which one makes meaningful eye contact with a whale or porpoise or some other creature who has heretofore never displayed consciousness, ensoulment.

"Vim and vinegar. That's no way to speak to your elders, my love. We three have inner and outer worlds the others know nothing about."

"I have no outer world. Get back to you about anything innerwise. I just know if I don't get some sleep this mastitis is going to set in, and I really don't want to be bleeding and blocked for the next few decades. We're so tired. Please."

The Crone steps up. She puts her hand on the Mother's cheek, kneads her fingers into her jaw.

"We know what we are, but know not what we may be," she whispers into the Mother's cheek.

The Crone presses her face to the Mother's forehead. Their tears form one stream, which merges and falls off the tributaries of the Crone's curled chin hairs like water spouts.

"Where have you been?" the Mother asks.

The Crone considers, knows she is not asking about this night.

"Grab the cauldron, my girls. It's past time we talked."

***

The three stand huddled around the gas stove. Flecks of glitter in the formica countertops reflect the blue, purple, white, orange of the flame.

The stove is the precise color of canned pea soup, thinks the Mother, who has been trying to place it for some time now.

The cauldron rests too-large, uneasily, on the front left burner.

"My girls, we are going to perform the ceremony. And I am going to tell you the truths. Maybe not in that order."

The Mother is staring into the empty pot, willing the abyss to finally pull her in, cook her down, mash her like apples. Finish feeding her to the universe.

"We must not perform the ceremony around fire," the Maiden says, alarmed.

"There are a lot of things we mustn't do," says the Crone. "I feel change on the wind, my loves... could also be distemperment of the stomach. Bit too much excitement lately, bit too much of the raw meat. But, I think it's change."

"Nothing ever changes," murmur the Mother and the Maiden in unison.

"Ah, but there's the rub. They want you to think that, the whole Administration. 'No' as a default is simple, simple, simple. They choke on change like an overcooked pork chop. S'why you've been feeding them a steady diet of your milk for these millenia," she says softly to the Mother, dipping a toe in the waters. "And you, feeding their egos, assuming their damage, thanking them for the privilege," she says to the Maiden. "And me, existing only when they need a disposable mystical meemaw, a sentient tree, a magical mammy, a spirit guide to salvation. A witch to burn. A point to prove about entrepreneurial old ladies."

She spits into the cauldron.

"I care for children. In the grandest of senses," the Mother says, hoarsely.

"And what do these children look like, exactly? What are their names, interests, dreams? Who are their mommies and daddies? Who are they to you? What do their heads smell like at night? Tell me about their spoiled milk-breath, how they snore like a muted flute. How you feel when they smile is the exact inverse of your terror for their safety. Tell me."

"You're asking questions without answers. They are... obscured to me," the Mother says, wishing the cauldron would boil over with images, details, emotions, anything, anything, to justify.

"It's the Wants I fill. If I don't, the children suffer. The world suffers. This you know."

"Go turn on the TV, my sweetheart."

The Maiden tiptoes to the television, turns the dial.

The image flickers, crackles, settles onto a reel of crowded, celebratory streets.

"People the world over fill the streets, in what can only be described as a tremendous display, while authorities continue the search for a person of interest. They ask the public's help. If you have any information, they request you call —"

The Mother's ears ring and her vision blurs.

The screen flashes to a grainy photograph, timestamped as from a security camera.

" —This is the image authorities have provided of the person of interest."

"It appears to be...now, what is that?" the co-anchor asks, overacting.

"It's being described as the person of interest's, um, knees."

"I've never seen knees like these," the co-anchor, who usually hosts the morning show, replies, slapping the anchor's back so hard his lapel mic shakes loose.

"Check your neighbors, everyone, for an old hag with molting legs. You may serve your country, if you don't toss your cookies first."

The co-anchor guffaws. Off-camera, the anchor, who has suppressed and sacrificed so much to retain his timeslot, glares at the clown next to him. The anchor considers who he was as a young, idealistic journalist, considers, not for the first time, of clawing back some integrity, almost releases the truth entrapped for so long behind his veneers —

Then again, he has the kids from the second marriage to put through prep school.

He bites his tongue, allows the idiot chirping to continue.

"Who weeps for these, weeps for corruption," the Crone recalls.

"Turn it off," the Mother whispers.

The Maiden watches the newscast, mouth agape, while the Crone, smiling, wipes a tear from her eye. She balances the droplet on her finger, makes her way to the cauldron, and drops it in.

Her tear sizzles, evaporates, bonds with the air.

"Yes, change," she says loudly, sniffing the vapors, waving them into her nose with her hand.

"Turn it off," the Mother shouts, making the Maiden jump. She turns the dial, having been trained since conception to honor the requests of those around her.

The television, for its part, fights its extinguishment with static and sputters, before it eventually goes black.

The Mother spins on her heel, strides to where the Crone is standing, eyebrows knitted, looking lovingly into the empty cauldron.

"For how long?" the Mother demands.

"Oh, goodness, you would ask that," the Crone says. "Hold on now, I can't think without my glasses."

The crone pats her pockets, front and back, takes out a pair of cardboard 3-D glasses, puts them on her face. They are wrinkled and fraying, a printed design of which the red stripes make her nose the vanishing point.

"You've been to a movie?" the Maiden demands, incredulous.

"Not since the French New Wave, my love. I've had quite a bit to catch up on, no time at all for the pictures."

"All this time, you've been living, letting us work ourselves to misery. Influencing world events? Why didn't you tell us?" the Mother demands.

"It's more of a collective manifestation than a direct influencing, really," her voice lilts "I've been experimenting, observing. Didn't want you girls to know until it was safe. I couldn't bear the thought of... what they'd do to you. They almost sniffed me out a few times, thought I was licked. First time, I missed an appointment to dispense some wisdom to a sad white child on a plantation. Broken toy or something. I was to sing a song and then smile, self-satisfied, while he ran across the horizon and I went back to churning my butter. Missed my cue — cartoon blue birds. Admin caught wind. I was assisting some folks by wagon across the Mason-Dixon up to Canada. It had a false bottom, see, and — now that I think about it, I do suppose I've been affecting lives just ever so teensy tiny."

She looks at the Mother, closing one eye and then the other, alternately peering through the red acetate, then the blue. She sees she is shaking with rage — or grief. One and the same, mostly, she thinks.

"...Sounds like they've finally got me, though, haven't they? I had a good long run... in several Olympics, even."

"It's not fair," the Maiden says after a long silence.

"No, honey, it's not."

"You still haven't answered my question," the Mother says.

"There is no good answer. Always. Never. Not so much, then a whole bunch. Once it was clear civilization wasn't going anywhere, I couldn't help m'self."

"When did you find the time?"

"People tend to ignore the elderly," the Crone says, pointedly. "Aside from my contractual obligations, nobody really seemed to notice where I was or what I was doing. Not least of which, you two. If the noose was up, and I've gotten into quite a few scrapes in my times, I must say," she chuckles, then stops abruptly, "I'd put myself in a bed or chair with a bib and drool a bit. Ask my grandchildren to visit, or the kids to call. You'd be surprised how quickly that makes people look away, stop asking questions, disappear entirely."

The Maiden stares at her wriggling toes. The Mother's eyes still burn.

"You could have taken us with you, sometimes," the Mother says through the lump in her throat.

"I could have. They'd have been onto us sooner, which is a risk I suppose we all could have agreed upon. I've been working on some things for posterity, my girls. And- I'm sorry for all that you've missed, and all that I had."

Without warning, the Crone lowers her head into her twisted hands and cries. When she lifts it again, finally, she wipes her nose on the sleeve of her t-shirt.

"There was a man once. And I chose him, and he chose me. And I loved him — oh my girls, I loved him. We were sanctified.

Equals. Put a stop to that, they did. Once you give — and receive — love, you get all sorts of ideas about what your life means. And you've paid the price for it too."

The Mother and the Maiden stand frozen, mouths agape.

"Now then, get your titties over here, there's work to be done," she says finally, hocking a ball of phlegm into the cauldron.

***

They stand, reunited, around the uneasy Cauldron on the burning stove.

"We beseech thee, let us rest," the Maiden begins.

"We offer thee the milk of our breasts," the Mother continues.

"The warmth of our worship," the Maiden says.

"The wisdom of ages," the Crone says.

"The fruits of our love, the kindly ones, we bear them for you, " they say in unison.

The mother nods to the maiden, who maneuvers her top off. Instinctually, she hunches over, curling her body into a question mark, goosebumps forming on her arms and torso.

Her bra is lacy, ill-fitting, covered in nonsensical bows and tassels. There are deep red depressions spreading from straps to skin.

"Go on, my sweetheart."

The Maiden reaches behind her back with both arms, fingers searching for the clasp. She winces, freezes, stands immobile for a minute too long. The others take note.

The Crone cranes her neck to look. She sees a swollen green-and-blue bruise which has spread between the Maiden's shoulder blades. She touches it as lightly as she can.

"Tell me."

"It doesn't matter."

"It very much matters."

"The appointment ran long. I needed to leave, for more reasons than one. That made him angry."

"I will do it for you, my love."

The Crone's rheumatic hands shake as she undoes the Maiden's clasp. She slides the straps off her shoulders without touching her skin, hands her the lingerie. It must be she who does it.

The Maiden takes the balled up bra in her fist.

"I give unto thee, so that I may rest," she says through gritted teeth.

She casts the bra into the cauldron. The flame melts the polyester into molten polymer sludge.

The Three choke on the fumes.

"Shouldn't we... the heat? They'll-" the Maiden says.

The Mother and the Crone shake their heads. The flame is necessary this time, will provide the activation energy. Bonds will break and bonds will form.

Bonds will burn this night.

The Mother unbuttons her top, allows it to slip from her fingers to the floor. Her nursing bra is yellowed, stained in the cups' apexes, stains no bleach can remove.

She reaches to undo the straps — left, then right, peeling the cups off her nipples. She pales with the pain.

Her exposed breasts are lumpy, swollen, scabbed. Scarred.

She undoes her clasp with one hand, tosses the nursing bra into the cauldron, where the absorbent cotton layers singe and smoke.

"I give unto thee, so that I may rest," she says through pained lips.

When she has composed herself, she locks eyes with the Crone.

The Crone sighs, whips off her t-shirt.

The Maiden and the Mother gasp as one.

The Crone wears nothing proudly.

"Where is it?" the Mother asks.

"Oh, um, it's... ah– around here somewhere."

The Maiden and Mother watch, unnerved, as the Crone rifles through cabinets, drawers, corners and crannies.

"Ah! Right where I left it," she says, finally, cradling an object with her back to her counterparts.

The Mother and Maiden sigh in relief.

The Crone turns to countenance the two and the cauldron. She holds a Tupperware container which is coated in greasy dust.

The Crone cracks the lid, presents the contents to the others, a child proud of her discovery, her captive.

She sniffs the air.

"Still fresh," she says, sadly. "Better for stew this way, though."

"Do I want to know how long that's been in there?" the Mother asks.

"What I'd like to know is how long you've been getting away with not wearing it," the Maiden snaps.

"Longer than you think; not long at all."

"Just put it in the pot already."

The Crone reaches the Tupperware over the pot, turns her arm, and dumps in an antique silk brassiere. The Mother sees, ever so quickly, the evidence of decades of armpit wet, spilled drinks, muddy splotches, running colors in the delicates load, back-breaking sweat, holes punched from wear.

The Crone stands on her toes, stares into the pot. She watches the silk burn slowly, retreat from the fire, release its fibers to oblivion.

"Smells like chicken," she says.

The Maiden grasps her by the elbow.

"Oughten't you say your part?" she asks.

"No, dear. I've been made to talk for so long. I'd like to listen now."

The Maiden makes desperate eye contact with the Mother.

Without the words, we cannot rest, she says with her irises. Without her conclusion, we are unfinished.

The Mother's face says, relax. It says, trust her. They listen to the singeing textiles, the melting fibers, the rising smoke that sings and smells of blood and hair and milk and tears.

"I'd like to say a few words after all," the Crone erupts.

"Go on then. They'll be waiting. They'll be listening."

"Philosopher, hiccup, nostalgia, teacup. Trivet, civet, banal divot. All done now, do you hear?" She cups her hands around her mouth in a megaphone and shouts into the pot, "All done now."

The Maiden furrows her brow while the Mother tosses her head back to belly laugh.

***

As the cotton and the silk and the poly blend solidify into an unnatural disc in the bottom of the Cauldron, the memories return.

It begins slowly at first, with the Mother witnessing fits and sprinkles of an ancient bacchanal. She sees herself lift a wrinkled arm to decant a flagon of wine directly into a young man's mouth.

The Maiden nestles under fur skins next to a warm body. Snowflakes fall onto her face, desire roils her core.

The Mother sits upon the stairs of a Gazebo in a town square, singing a song about following one's dreams to a group of gathered children.

The Maiden grips an iron gate, rust piercing her tender palms.

The Mother leads a conquering capitalist through a sunlit forest trail. He can have it all, she explains, if only he knew the curves of the creek as the curves of her body.

The Maiden cradles a child, smells her hair, her spoiled milk breath, presses her lips to her cheek, the most perfect to exist.

The Mother stands on a balcony, lets the wind work her hair loose as she lights a cigarette, watches the tip burn, lets it singe a curl.

The Maiden stands, walks, drops her keys and badge on her supervisor's desk, says, I quit.

The Mother cries into the chest of a man, who buttresses her with his arms.

ARIA FOR A GRASSHOPPER

"You remember all because we have never been Three," says the Crone. "And now, we are free."

***

A rotary phone rings incessantly, insistently, on the kitchen wall.

The neighbors have complained for weeks, to no avail. The landlord finds himself entirely unable to access the dwelling, an excuse the other tenants find insulting, untenably dishonest.

But, the man is not lying.

He has tried everything: breaking the glass, sawing a hole in the attic's floor, employing some volunteer firefighters-in-training to use the Jaws of Life on the door.

They too have inexplicably failed, and the apartment remains inaccessible. They will tell their incredulous buddies about it over drinks at the sports bar that night, will be dismissed as having inhaled too much smoke on a call.

I swear to you, he says to the tenants, there is no landline. We have cut every wire.

There is no way in.

The only solution may be total condemnation, though that will certainly hurt his bottom line. He avoids the inevitable for as long as humanly possible.

The phone remains ringing.

Then, one day, when the building's tenants are preparing to move, filling boxes, cursing their ineffectual noise-cancelling headphones, popping paracetamol like candy for the exhaustion headache, the phone stops ringing.

They can't quite believe it at first, as their ears have substituted a phantom ringing for the real thing.

They sit in the silence for a long time as their bodies adjust to reality.

It is true, the ringing has stopped.

One of them gets the crazy idea that perhaps the apartment is unlocked, and they enter as a small army of investigators, of "just what the hell has been going on here after all."

They squeeze through the door, filing one by one into the kitchen, which is the only room that appears to be fully spared from the continuous-form paper exploding from, what — a fax machine? — which is buried somewhere deep in the apartment.

One of the tenants sidles to the ecru rotary phone on the wall, which floats in his vision, a summoning sun, against the encroaching white paper mass.

He picks it up. There is a dial tone.

"Hello?" he says.

"Who's this?" a Voice demands on the other end.

"Uh-uh, you first, buddy. I got a room full of people here who would like to know what the hell is going on here, why we haven't slept for a goddamn month."

"Are they there?"

"Yeah, the whole goddamn building is here."

"Not them."

"Who are you, anyway? I've got a mind to call the cops. Let them question you. This place is a tinder box, and I think you know something about it, not to mention the harassing calls."

"I'm Tom. Where are they?"

"Dunno. Haven't seen *them* since —"

"That's all. Hang up the phone now."

"Yeah, well, fuck you too, buddy."

The neighbor slams the receiver down hard enough to shatter the phone.

"Let's go," he says to the others. "We ain't gettin' no answers. But at least we can get back to our lives."

As the neighbors squeeze back out of the kitchen, out the door, and down the steps one-by-one, a little girl picks up a loose scrap of paper, which has been folded into an origami lotus flower.

Of course the grown-ups don't notice these things, certainly not when they blend into the surroundings, but she is always on the lookout for signs and signals from the fairy realm.

The little girl goes back to her bedroom next door, sits on a pile of boxes which her mother has instructed her to unpack, and unfolds the paper lotus flower.

The note reads in a shaky and curled hand: "Forever and forever farewell! Gone to IHOP. Don't tell Tom."

The little girl scowls, reads the note three times.

She decides it is a practical joke, as fairies are wont to play. Or some kind of code.

She puts the note in her dresser drawer for later, resumes a pretend saga with her three favorite dolls.

Her mother will discover, read, re-place the strange note the next time she puts away the child's laundry.

Such a fascinating imagination that child has; she'll use her powers for good someday, she thinks.

IV. Womanhood

"Mother, you must free your kind."

In the Garden, We Kill Boys

Mary tightens her grip on the damp iron gate. She feels rust crumble under the pressure of her hand. She enjoys the alchemy of its melting from porous corrosion to a painterly red paste in her palms.

Blood on her hands, so to speak.

She surveys her surroundings. Night-time, but the moon's glow upon the fog's veil gives the appearance of dusk rather than midnight. Ancient privet hedges have grown tall and lush, twisted on opposite sides of the fence, thriving in their independence, in reclamation of this small slice of earth.

ARIA FOR A GRASSHOPPER

Through the gate, she can see the garden's verve barely contained- roses, the color of blood and sunset, reaching towards the sky, outmaneuvering the creeping nightshade below. The birch and the dogwood and the cherry branches reach for each other, entangling themselves in a slithering, silent battle for sunlight. The beech branches, their bark glowing a lush velvet gray from within, observe the scene from a haughty distance on high. The garden breathes, perfumes the air with its exhalations.

Mary squeezes the gate harder as her cheeks flush and her extremities surge with blood.

She closes her eyes and rolls her head, stretching her neck, enjoying the release. She groans a bit in the back of her throat at the indignity of aging muscles and aching bones under still-smooth skin. She pauses with her head bowed in prayer position, hands still firmly clasped upon the gate.

C. G. RENNIE

A sharp finger raps Mary's shoulder.

Mary startles, spins around, comes face to face with another woman.

"Enjoying yourself, were you?" the woman says.

Mary, heart galloping, grunts.

She does not release the gate from her left hand's grip, a defensive posture that might not save her, but at least give anchor to kick and scream.

The woman is older than Mary — not by much.

She sports practical, outdoorsy clothing, hair pulled back. Rebellious gray flyaways. Freckles like reverse constellations. Professor of Anthropology, if Mary had to guess.

If you held a knife to her throat.

An ally, no doubt, having just fed her sourdough starter, chose her expensive walking shoes and corporate-liberal zip-up to wear on this night. But what would one wear to such a thing, anyway? Come dressed in one's best Stevie Nicks cosplay?

"Just taking in the night air," Mary says, raising an eyebrow, a signal, should the other woman understand it. Mary's stomach lurches at the risk.

She never did have much of a poker face, either.

"Relax," the woman says. "We can walk together. They'll be waiting."

Mary narrows her eyes, chews the inside of her cheek. Trust isn't her default mode. Then again, she doesn't know, in all practical senses, where she's going, only has the vaguest sense of what to do when she gets there.

"Chop chop," the woman says, reading her mind.

Mary attempts to open the gate, throwing her whole weight behind it. No dice.

The woman, who is taller than she, reaches above Mary's hands, gripping the same bars, trapping Mary from behind.

The moment to strike, if she means to.

The gate whines, indignant, fighting against every millimeter of progress they make.

The gate prefers stasis, having been built to preserve the status quo, and having become — as all fences, walls, and barriers do- more conservative with age.

The women work together, work up a sweat, until the gate has sufficiently seen things their way.

Mary quivers as she struggles through the gap. She feels the other woman's amused gaze, which roils the anger and anxiety already percolating in her chest. Mary's temper, her lashing out, is a certain factor in what led her here, but this is a calculated mission.

Mustn't lose our heads.

Halfway through the gap, the latch pressing between her shoulder blades like a loaded gun, Mary turns her head to glare at her companion.

The woman stares back, impassively, unconcerned, no difference to her whether she or anyone else gets in — or out — on this lovely midnight stroll.

Mary bites at her cheek and sucks in her belly, tucks her butt, scrapes her back against the rough iron.

The hem of Mary's coat catches on an ornamental swirl, an iris or lily or lotus or oleander, but who could say after decades of decay, paint, rust and rain. Mary yanks hard at the hem, panic flaring in her stomach; a dizzy, blurred fog descends upon her head.

She tears herself free; the velocity throws her to the ground, pebbles sticking to her rust-bloodied hands like craggy stigmata.

Pull yourself together, she thinks; *this isn't even the hard part*, she thinks.

***

The other woman watches Mary struggle, bemused at the first-timer's nerves. She had felt that way once. The woman recalls the electric alert of the ceremony, the power of the cosmic contained within: first, a hard, green bud, then, as a feathery bloom, and finally, a luxuriant, decaying brown.

Supplantation, supplementation. Retribution.

She knows her flippancy is irritating her companion. This is deliberate.

It cannot be done without anger, without some proverbial and literal dirt under the fingernails, without some wounding.

The larva must always resent its cocoon enough to destroy it.

***

Mary picks the pebbles from her palms and sets herself to rights. She darts her eyes in the direction from whence she has come: blacktop, sidewalk, yellow lines, nothing.

She opens her mouth to call out, to warn the others of an intruder, of betrayal, sabotage, abortive genesis.

A smug face comes into focus.

"Let's go," Mary hisses at her. "We could be seen."

The woman rolls her eyes and elegantly slips through the gate, as if she could expand and contract at will, as if the limitations of physics were simply a matter of discretion.

She extends her hand, pulls Mary up brusquely, aggressively, despite the disarming softness of her touch.

Mary locks eyes with the woman once they are at level. The woman returns her gaze with an inscrutable expression — compassion? Or, alarmingly: pity.

The woman, feeling exposed, turns away, begins to stride down the gravel path.

Mary says, with all the softness she can muster, "Wait."

She points to the chips of rust and black paint that have settled on the ground outside the gate. Anyone monitoring the area would know someone has entered the garden recently. Their footprints are ground into the dirt.

The other woman purses her lips in concession. Yes, it is still best to be prudent. Though she is beyond fear at the moment, she understands practical measures.

After all, that's why she's here.

The women move in tandem, using dirt to cover their tracks, branches to rake the pebbles smooth. Fingers extend through black and decaying bars to pluck the detritus carefully away.

At the moment of execution, they begin their pilgrimage.

***

The fog is growing denser as the dark hours tick past.

ARIA FOR A GRASSHOPPER

Good, Mary thinks; *Nature holding up its end of the bargain thus far.*

Once they are sufficiently deep into the garden's interior, out of earshot from outsiders, the woman speaks.

"So, who are you tonight?"

Mary pauses to consider.

"You can call me 'Mary.'"

The woman stops, swivels her head to get another good look at Mary, her lips thawing into a frown of reconciled approval.

"If you're the Mary, you can call me Magdalena."

The woman smiles conspiratorially. She squeezes Mary's bicep once, twice.

Mary snatches her arm from Magdalena's grasp, hating her for her familiarity, for her faith, so easily given.

"Oh, lighten up," Magdalena says. "I was you not so long ago — so to speak. Other than the backache you'll have tomorrow, it's not so bad."

She pauses. "And, if the others are good at what they're doing, it can actually be quite a release."

Magdalena wiggles her eyebrows. Mary scowls, runs her tongue over her teeth.

Mary marches forward, but not before Magdalena clocks her smirk.

Maybe this one has a sense of humor after all, Magdalena thinks. *It'd be a long night without.*

***

Mary takes in the garden as they make their way along the pea-gravel path. It appears, at one time, to have been a public park of sorts, or more likely, the private playground, modeled after a hodgepodge of European styles, a substitution for noble blood and ancient breeding, for some Robber Baron of yore, which had been donated to the public land trust to preserve his legacy after death, so that the citizenry would remember him for his libraries and museums and gardens and solariums and train stations instead of their own exploitation, and then left to ruin as the wealthy fled this part of the city, tax dollars dried up, those seeking home, refuge, moved in, dared enjoy the spoils of the shade and fruit trees without the proper permitting or bank balance, dared escape their suffering with pharmaceutical assistance, until the city surrounded the garden with chain link and padlocks, warning signs, arrests, and razor wire, when the rest didn't work.

Circle of life stuff.

Nonetheless, Mary enjoys the scenery.

Privets shoot out their branches as far as they wish, revelling in freedom from pruning, from clips and snips at the hands of man.

Moss grows on twisted tree roots which have risen above the earth.

They say, *Trip on me. I won't feel sorry.*

The remains of old wooden benches dotting the landscape are rotten, slimy, collapsed in the middle, home to worms and termites and fire ants. The odd bit of styrofoam.

ARIA FOR A GRASSHOPPER

The wood gurgles a sigh of relief as the women walk past without molesting it with their bottoms, the pollution of their poly blends. Old resentments dying hard, and all that.

Wrinkled leaves sprout from the ground, taking their sweet time to unfurl their perennial displays, sharing their beauty with their own, when and how they wish.

Sure, someone put us here, our seeds were transported over oceans against our will, but we make the rules now, they say. *We'll flourish as we please, fuck you very much indeed.*

Mary barely registers a fork in the path, focusing instead on the widow's peak of a hemlock grove. She strains to see the trunks in the shadows, whose ichthyotic, superannuated bark is lined with crevasses and canyons.

They form cartoon faces in the night, as if a black and white, jangly-limbed skeleton whistling animated music notes might step out from behind, to guide them.

"Not that way," Magdalena says.

"What?"

"Left at the fork, not right. Always left. Never right."

"Oh, okay. Right."

"No, left."

"Do you enjoy being this irritating? Like, all the time."

"Maybe I should have gone by 'Karen' tonight."

"Oh my god, just walk ahead of me, and I'll follow you."

Magdalena saunters in front of Mary, walks too slowly, so that Mary is constantly stepping on the backs of her shoes.

"You're hurting me," Magdalena says, child-like.

Mary squalls loud enough to scare a pair of doves, who abandon their ground nest, replete with their young, for the safety of height.

The doves watch as the invasive species engage in a strange courting ritual: one racing in front of the other, pulling her hair, screeching, falling back, repeat repeat repeat, until they have turned the bend of the old pea-gravel path and are out of sight.

The doves regard each other, then flit simultaneously back down to the nest, where their young scold them for their temporary fright, the almost-danger, the exercise in character- building.

***

Deeper into the trees, Magdalena is crooning under her breath.

"Mary, Mary, quite contrary, how does your garden grow? With silver bells and cockle shells and silver maids all in a row."

The women have ceased hair-pulling, having finally settled into the silent treatment when they remembered themselves in a small clearing.

Things were going well this way, until Magdalena chose petty annoyance as violence. As she very well knows.

"Mary, Mary, quite contrary, how does your garden grow? With silver bells and cockle shells and silver maids all in a row."

Operatically now. Mary wouldn't admit it, even under duress, but she has a nice set of pipes.

Mary plods ahead to escape the sonic assault, slips on a rock, feels the rage growing in her belly as her knee swells and her scrapes ooze blood.

Do not cry, she thinks. *Do not cry. Don't give her the satisfaction.*

"Mary, Mary, Mary, quite contrary... about those cockles though," Magdalena says at full volume, "and all those silver maids."

And then, she cackles.

The audacity.

Mary, half-limping, runs, shoves Magdalena into a topiary hedge, pins her against it, Magdalena's arms splayed, roaring with laughter. Mary pushes her harder into the brush, wishes she could push her clean through to the other side, but shutting her up will have to do.

Magdalena is fully entangled with the bush. She has a cut on her cheek, weeping blood. The woman is finally, blessedly, silent. Mary holds her down, though Magdalena does not struggle.

Her eyes are clear and present. Enlightened, even.

Mary's own eyes follow the blood as it slides down Magdalena's cheek.

Crying her heart out, poor thing, inanimate icon, arms wide to the world.

"Go on," says Magdalena, soberly, softly. "You need every bit you can get. The anger, that helps too."

Mary begins to release her grip on Magdalena's arms. The world is going white, like low blood sugar on a hot day.

She lets go with one hand, reaches into her pocket for the bitter little pill she tucked in there for just such an emergency.

"No," Magdalena says, as to a puppy. "Do it."

Mary glares at her, if not hungrily, then at least peckish.

"That's disgusting," she says.

"What are you here for, then?" Magdalena says, cocking her head to the side, yet somehow not patronizing.

Mary closes her eyes, edges her lips to Magdalena's bloody cheek. She holds out her tongue, allowing the droplets to fall onto it. At least, she thinks, it's just gravity responsible for the contact between foreign blood and yearning maw.

Until she swallows.

That, she'd have to take full responsibility for, knowing full well she will crack under questioning about all of tonight, every single detail, like the little weakling tattletale she is.

Magdalena laughs and pushes Mary away from her. Mary wipes at her lips with her sleeve, ashamed.

"Oh, don't do that. You'll offend me," Magdalena says.

Her hair has fallen loose from the attack. It's much longer than Mary expected. Ringlets materialize around her shoulders.

Magdalena wiggles her way out of her jacket, which has become entangled in the topiary. Underneath, she is wearing a thin, impractical camisole, her nipples hard from the cold.

"Let's go, Mary," emphasis on *Mary*. "They'll be waiting."

Magdalena grabs Mary by the hand, uses her leverage to hoist herself out of the hedge's grasp. Her grip is still strong, resolved.

Mary pulls Magdalena in and kisses her, hard. The women fall into a nearby pile of creeping phlox, their hair intertwining with opportunistic rose bushes.

Magdalena, lips flushed, rolls away from Mary, sits up, dusts herself off.

"Save it, Mary."

She cracks her neck.

She yanks her jacket from a pilfering rosebush; it has won the tug-of-war with the enemy hedge — and why not, with thorns as thick as fingers and a reach as long as its ambition?

Magdalena shrugs back into her jacket. Mary watches, bewildered.

"This isn't about me. Or all that," Magdalena waves her hand erratically in Mary's direction, emphasis on *that*. "It just means it's all working. That it's going to work."

She laughs.

"You slut. You're probably not even gay in real life."

***

When the women reach their destination, Mary is shocked to see a festival-like crowd in the middle of the clearing.

She surveys the area: seven paths, radiating from one circular point: in the middle, a lone Bradford Pear tree.

It emanates semen and death, a carrion loneliness, no female to mate with, yet another miscalculation by the men who planted it.

No fruit. No future. A synecdoche of impotence.

"All paths led here after all," says Magdalena, before receding into the crowd, fluttering her fingers at Mary as both 'hello' and 'goodbye.'

Mary turns her attention to the gathered. Women of all races, ages, and assignments-at-birth mingle, sharing a drink, sharing a laugh, sharing a meal. Sharing a purpose. Some are napping in the crooks of willows and poplars and sycamores; some are familiarizing themselves with each other in darker corners of the clearing.

Children play despite the darkness of the hour, being neither in danger nor in want of any number of loving mothers and aunties, no monsters, no wolves waiting behind the next tree, the strangers with candy and only the gentlest intentions.

When the crowd spots Mary walking toward the Bradford Pear tree at the center of the circle, silence descends. No one has yet crossed the stones.

She pauses at the precipice. Waits.

Unsure why she is here, she studies the tree: bark, blossoms, branches, fecundity, as if she were scrutinizing a museum object.

As if her life depended on it.

It is a scourge on the garden, and it must be purged.

***

It was planted here sometime in the middle of the twentieth century, during a fit of post-war urban renewal on this side of town. Some city official, taking a shit, shifting his hairy ass on the padded plastic seat, cursing the ubiquitous, inescapable doilies his wife has swathed the whole goddamn house in, can't a man just take a constitutional without lace covering every visible surface, without ribbons on the toilet paper holder, this is my great-grandfather's brownstone, not a chintzy fairy palace, goddamn sewing circle nonsense, at least it keeps her out of my hair, had seen a picture of a Bradford Pear tree in some home and garden magazine of his wife's, the newspaper being out of reach on the kitchen table, blooming and beautiful, lined up and planted in parallel rows as far as the lens could capture and beyond, straddling the streets of a new-build suburban paradise like milky white dominoes.

Tidy, orderly. White as far as the eye could see.

The kind of community that attracted the expatriates from this part of town, commuting back and forth to the city every day like some sort of idiot geese migration, leaving the opening for a more invasive species to take up residence in their abandoned townhouses and walk-ups.

And while this particular city official did not believe that the introduction of the Bradford Pear alone would be responsible for the neighborhood's restoration to its Gilded Age glory days per se, gall-darn it, it was certainly an (economical) step in the right direction.

People need a symbol to get behind. A gathering place, preferably of the photogenic varietal. Not this gaudy Technicolor means of reflecting the world back at itself; he prefers a dignified image in black and white, clear lines, strong borders, push the darks back into the shadows where they belong.

Perhaps his picture would be featured in a magazine someday, heck, the whole family in *Better Homes and Gardens*, centered between two rows of flowering pear trees, the five — or six of them, if he has his way — positioned in front of the vanishing point, the All-American ideal, huge white smiles gleaming, thank you so very much for letting us come, daddy, no, I think hat off, in this case, sir, it's no matter that the sun is reflecting that halo around your shiny skull, while other families just like his picnic amongst the blooms, the wives leering at him as their husbands lift their own little sprouts up by their fat thighs to pick ripe, juicy pears, and thank you sir, for bringing some sanity back to city planning, and well, I'll just go ahead and say it, giving the neighborhood a good 'ole Ivory scrubbing, if you catch my meaning.

So when this particular city official approached his superior on Monday with the idea, his boss laughed in his face, a man with no vision, no interest, except when a new secretary caught his eye, except when his palms itched from lack of greasing, said he'd find the funds for one measly tree, and tell you what, you can even plant it yourself like some pinko beatnik, finally get your hands dirty for a change, goddamn goodie-two-shoes over here, and on your way out, ask whatever-her-name-is to come on in, I have something that needs lookin' over, if you catch my meaning.

And so it was that this particular city official was digging a hole with an old, dull municipal shovel, deep enough for the root ball of the lone Bradford Pear tree he was afforded. No picnickers, no press, no adoring family, I planted a tree today, kids, that's nice dad, but can we go back to *Howdy Doody* already, why'd you call us out here to tell us that? Darn it all, Dwight, why are your fingernails so dirty? You're fudging up the armchair doilies with that filth, and I just had the girl starch and press them, you know how much I have to hover just to get the help to do one gall-darn thing right, those people being naturally predisposed to tolerating filth, just a man in the hot sun and a white button down, respectable tie, grinding dirt into the knees of his slacks for the betterment of his community, going unappreciated.

He had selected the most famous section of the garden, at the intersection of all things, the center of attention, the impetus for renewal would radiate out in seven directions, when really it just ended up being the gall-darn stink in the spring, enough to make you gag, enough to keep people away from that part of the park altogether, like sweat and sin, like a hooker's trap, his boss said, laughing until he wheezed, had a coughing fit, yelled for the girl to come in and show him how to work this goddamn inhaler again, moron doctors and their modern cures.

He had leaned up against the wobbly, skinny sapling, once it was in the ground, to catch his breath, imagining future generations doing the same, the writers and poets and pictures that would be inspired by the tree's shade, the re-birth of a nation, under God, forever and ever, Amen.

Symbols being what they are, malleable things — one man's proud heritage being another man's reminder of his place in the grand order of things, the way they ought to be — the city official had briefly considered that perhaps his ambitions were too limited. Perhaps it should have been a statue of a great general of yore, trees being too of-the-land and ambiguous in their intent.

Too open to interpretation.

Still, the value of an honest day's labor. That should count for something.

His knees cracked as he stood, brushed the dirt best he could from his slacks, Alba better have dinner on the table tonight before she disappears to euchre, always coming home reeking of gin and Shalimar, unseemly for a lady and mother, unacceptable, really, when he spends his own days doing man's work.

God's honest work.

***

Mary crosses the stone circle, turns around to face the crowd.

The faces are all materially unfamiliar, arrangements of colors and shapes, expressions and histories she has never seen in her life, and yet —

The women form a circle around Mary, remaining just on the other side of the tree's stone border.

A woman with gray flyaways and sensible walking shoes makes eye contact with Mary, sips from a teacup, strokes the head of a child who has snuggled against her. The child is wearing bell-bottom corduroys, pigtail braids, tight curls peeking out from under the securing ribbons. The freckles on her skin are mirrored constellations of the woman's nestling her.

The child smiles warmly at Mary. Mary waves to the girl as if she had spotted a friend from across the street. The girl giggles, hides her face in the woman's jacket.

The woman takes a final gulp, hands her teacup to someone; it is absorbed into the crowd. She swallows, sighs, and steps forward to join Mary across the border, evidently the designated emissary.

Her expression is somewhat sheepish, sympathetic. She takes Mary's hands in hers.

"Hi, Mary," she says. "I don't suppose you remember me." Her tone is that of a nurse speaking to a dementia patient.

Mary studies her face. The woman has a cut, some freshly dried blood on her cheek.

She shakes her head, no, I'm sorry, I don't know you.

"That's all right," the woman says. "I didn't expect you would. The path here... it can take you out of your head."

The crowd titters at this.

Mary overhears someone whisper, "I stomped off for a bit because this one —" she gestures with her thumb to the woman next to her, "kept threatening to ask out my crush on my behalf. Wouldn't drop it."

The woman next to her grimaces, mouths: *sorry*.

"Took me forever to get here. My shoes didn't match my outfit, allegedly. Kept hiding so no one would see me," someone replies from the back.

The crowd titters again, sharing accounts of their own garden passage, laughing, guffaws, heads back, heads down, pats on the back, tears in their eyes, holding one another up, releasing.

"The voices told me I didn't belong. My body, it-," a tall woman wails with all the force of her primal being.

And the multitude forms a band around her, chanting, *you are here, you belong, you are here, you are right where you belong*.

When the crowd quiets, settles into a simmer, an old woman steps forward into the circle.

She is thin, skin like an impasto painting, waves upon waves. Her hair is wild, white, electrified. She wears a faded and fraying flannel shirt, sleeves rolled up to her elbows, worn cut-off shorts, exposing knees like tree rings, and a yellowing, holey t-shirt that reads "7th Annual Barbecue Cook-Off, Levittown, NY" with a crudely-drawn, steaming pot of the same, both the letters and the image cracked and peeling.

A few of her more robust chin hairs gleam in the moonlight.

"That old pubescent rage needs to age a bit to be useful," she says to Mary, whose bewilderment is evident. She pats Mary on the cheek, worrying her fingers into Mary's tense jaw. She feels the divots in the tips of the old woman's fingers, the weight she carries in her swollen knuckles, the twists of her fingers like the most ancient of branches.

"But what would an old crone like me remember about all that? I hit the menopause somewhere between the first and seventh Caesar. Not as shit as the one before him — pretty low bar there, but he didn't last long, either."

The Crone draws a line across her throat, drops her tongue out of her mouth and gurgles.

She jerks her jangly limbs a couple times for emphasis.

"Anyway," says the Crone, "you ready to deliver?"

"I thought I was here to cut down a- a tree," says Mary.

"Bit of this, bit of that."

ARIA FOR A GRASSHOPPER

***

Mary picks up the axe, steeling her grip on the old wooden handle. There are worn-in grooves from other hands, other gatherings, the handle smoothed from use across time and distance. The head of the axe shines in the moonlight, having been sharpened and oiled by loving hands this night.

Her hands are sore, what with various wounds and abrasions, though she can't recall how her palms came to be this way. Like waking up from a deep sleep with mysterious bruises, only the faintest recollection of a savage nightmare.

The Crone has stepped back into the crowd. She is watching Mary, arms crossed, hip jutted out, lips pursed, as if to say, *Let's get this show on the road, it's past my bedtime.*

The other woman — she has been instructed to call her Magdalena — has remained inside the circle with Mary.

"Spread your legs, keep your knees soft," she croons to Mary like a doula. "That's it. Now, adjust your grip, spread your fingers. Tighten. Good."

Mary follows the woman's directions, finds herself getting lost in her rhythm, her incantation.

"Breathe. When you swing, exhale. Keep on like that until it's done," Magdalena murmurs.

In her periphery, Mary sees that the women have closed in tighter, to each other and to her. They are swaying as one, humming a familiar song Mary can't place, like a radio playing in a dream, but she's awake — she thinks, anyway, though who in their waking life would be cutting down a stinking tree in the middle of a shuttered city park, encircled by a klatsch of gardening enthusiasts?

For what purpose, love? a boy in the back of her memory asks, reciting from rote, flat, unenthused.

Mary lets the axe drop. It hangs, no less certain of its personal role in the matter, at her side.

Magdalena is unphased. Patience is key, and they have all night. She positions her face between Mary's gaze and her navel.

Mary mumbles something.

"What?"

"This is insanity," she repeats.

"Probably," says Magdalena.

"I can't believe I got talked into it."

"Have some faith?"

"Ha."

"I won't bother with any 'chosen one' nonsense. Frankly, any one of us could assume your position, do the thing, and we'd all be back in our beds sooner. Just a job that needs doing is all; you so happen to be the doer this time. We're talking a few inches — twelve, maybe fifteen, he's a bit girthy," she grins while Mary rolls her eyes, "of a stinky old tree trunk that stands between us and," she raises her eyebrows at Mary, knows Mary knows what she knows.

"How stupid," says Mary. "As if."

"A chance," finishes Magdalena.

"Plenty and peace breeds cowards; hardness ever of hardiness is mother," erupts the Crone.

"That's right, Mama!" yells someone from the crowd. The gathered whisper in assent.

"Whatever that means," says Mary.

"That 3 A.M. feeling, Mary. It wasn't nothing. We all woke up, knew it, felt each other feel it, sensed down to our blood and bones that time had shifted, reality had split into wrong and right had disintegrated, that fragile little string finally broke. Didn't need to look at our phones, because we already knew. We're on the wrong thread, Mary. Time to cut dead weight loose. We start binding it all back together, now."

Mary looks around at the faces of the gathered. She heaves the axe up, rests it on her shoulder.

"I — what if it doesn't work?"

"Then all you'll have done is created a new ecosystem in the literal sense. Given the carpenter ants a new McMansion with a three-car garage."

"The natural order of things," she pauses, "is what we say it is. Inhale, swing, exhale," says Magdalena. "Clean strokes. No debating with it. Don't try to reason with it. Don't let it sucker you. Just because it's gotten to where it is doesn't mean it deserves to be."

"I begin to find an idle and fond bondage in the oppression of aged tyranny, who sways, not as it hath power, but as it is suffered," recalls the Crone, tapping her finger to her temple. "And that's coming from my old ass. Besides, the thing stinks to heaven of fish milt and dirty balls. He's gotta go. I already missed my *Cheers* reruns. I won't be missing *Wings*," she finishes, with an edge of threat.

Mary squares her shoulders, takes a couple slow practice swings for aim — and then, she lets fly.

The women sing and sway while Mary swings, eating away at the trunk. She is increasingly aware, with every stroke, every connective fiber that is severed, every creak and moan — from her lips to goddess' ears — of her blood surging throughout her body, of a small, hard bud that has formed, stretched, bloomed, released, rotted, each step in the sequence more glorious than the last. Each swing, less and less effort and more emancipation, less lone endeavor and more common aspiration.

A regeneration by way of extermination.

The tree falls. The gathering is here to see it, to mark it, and the women exhale as one.

Release? Relief.

Mary cries out, collapses to the ground. Magdalena rushes to her, takes her pulse, *maybe not Anthropology, maybe nursing*, thinks Mary nonsensically, as much as she can string thoughts together at the moment. She splays her arms and legs wide with abandon, begins making snow angels in the pea-gravel path, the trunk of the felled tree looking for all the world like a new appendage from all angles of observation.

"She's fine," announces Magdalena. "Just enjoying herself."

"Good for you, Mama!" someone shouts from the back.

Blessed be, they chant until they disperse back to their lives, some together, some alone, trickling away into the garden, "See you at the next one," they say, "Oh, you know me, baby, I don't miss a liquidation…"

Seven paths splitting into one shared future.

Only Mary, returned to reality from the realm of her senses, Magdalena, and the Crone remain, overseeing the scene.

The Crone marches to the remains, her ringed knees a trick reflection of the fallen stump's concentric layers.

She straddles the trunk.

"Le petit mort," she says. "Fuck 'em."

***

Many miles away, across rivers and oceans and mountains and valleys, an old man lies in his palace bedroom. He dreams the unconscionably restful sleep of an authoritarian with unbound power and absent virtue.

His father was a mid-level city official at one time or another, a bald loser, lived his whole life in his father's father's father's ugly old brownstone, in the old neighborhood, the old country, clung to it while it all went to shit, last rat standing on that sinking ship, mom, a drunk with a bouffant and a penchant for frills of all sorts — decor, drinks, the few perquisites she could convince her husband to partake in on the community's behalf. Waste not, want not. Father wanted his funeral in front of a stinking tree in that dump of a public garden. His team had had to scour the area for used needles, lest one of his children injure themselves, toss a couple under the ex-wives' assigned seats, would ya? I'm joking, whores've already got every disease known to man and junkie alike. Yeah, this is the old neighborhood, a real beaut, huh? But I had some good times here, behind that crumbling bandstand, if you catch my meaning. 'Course you do, they're all willing.

Every single one.

Dreaming, he wanders the hallways of a building he concludes is an alma mater. It does not resemble any school he attended — and there were many — in any physical manner he could verbalize, though admittedly, conceptual relational communication is difficult for this man, as it would require him to recognize other people as equally human.

He tips himself off: this is a dream, have some fun, my boy.

He is increasingly aware, however, of a looming final exam, a nagging test he is late for, a class he has not attended all semester.

No worries, he tells himself, as absolution will come from one phone call from his father, is one doctor's note away, one coded call from code enforcement.

Evidently, fun is as hard to find here in dreams as it was in reality: one had to make his own fun.

Blessings of blessings, a group of girls pass him in the hallway, all uniforms and loafers and laughter.

He spins on his heel and follows them into the lavatory.

At first, they laugh uncomfortably, in an attempt to keep things light.

He continues to edge in closer to them, until their backs are against the wall. It is the growing fear, the dropping of formalities and pretense he has always enjoyed. The satisfaction as the veil between the subtext and the inevitability falls.

"Just a little bit," he says. "I won't tell anyone. Or maybe I will, if it's not any good."

He pins the smallest girl to the wall, well aware that this is a dream, it isn't real, he can do as he pleases — that is, without paying anyone off, shutting anyone up, convincing his parents yet again that the rumors couldn't possibly be true, who are you going to believe? Your own son, or some scholarship slut/ intern/ secretary/ counter girl/ housekeeper/ ex-wife/ stranger from the wrong side of town?

The girl begins crying while her friends punch and kick at him, which only excites him more.

He tries to get a good look at the girl's face, the better to recollect when he needs a boost during waking hours, but the only clear features are the widened eyes, the streaming tears, the hair matted with wet to her cheeks.

He fumbles with his zipper. Why is everything so goddamn difficult in dreams? Like wading through water with weights on your limbs. For a brief moment, he prefers his waking life without obstacles, without the weight of consequence.

He averts his gaze from the crying girl's face to his ineffectual fingers. In the darkness of the corner, where the grimy fluorescent lighting can't penetrate, he can't make out his malfunctioning hands.

He releases the girl momentarily to lift his hands to his face. They are covered in warts, which are expanding exponentially, growing like tree limbs, fusing his bones together into a mass of ichthyotic bark, cutaneous horns sprouting like wrinkled spring leaves along the length of his arms.

He screams, though no sound escapes his lips.

The girl's friends step back in horror, then they are laughing and pointing, laughing until the tears stream down their faces, doubling over, all the while the mutation is spreading until he is solely a face inside a rotting, warty, festering, stinking tree which has sprouted from the sickly citrine floor tiles.

The smallest girl steps forward. Her features are clear as day now.

He recognizes her, could tell you exactly when and where, which dormitory/ supply closet/ locked office/ dressing room/ pantry/ vacation home/ parking garage.

Except the faces aren't exhibiting the telltale signs of distress. They look — what is it? — triumphant, exhilarated.

Exalted.

Her faces cycle again and again and again as he struggles to wake himself up.

Back in reality, his body is paralyzed, but for the tiniest of tremors, but for the occasional whimper, which goes unheard.

Her faces settle, merge, converge into one: an old woman, skin like melted wax, chin hairs sparkling in the light radiating from inside her.

He rages at her ugliness, the audacity to exist fully in her form, to think nothing of putting this face, with its wrinkles and lines, scars and scabs, moles and maddening confidence in all righteousness in front of his own, of her unmistakable expression of imminent victory.

The Crone smiles at him, wide and toothy.

She is so close, he can see the vertical lines in her coffee-stained teeth, the linear sensuousness of their infinite experiences: the lovers they have grazed, the bones she has gnawed upon, enemies whose flesh she has torn off and spat out.

He cannot move, cannot turn his head, cannot close his eyes; the bark has supplanted his eyelids, refuses to bend to his will.

"Say it," the Crone says.

"Say what? What do you want, you nasty old bitch? Let me wake up."

"You know very well what to say."

"No."

"Strange...talking has never been your problem. You talk and talk and talk, don't you? And look where it's gotten you. Incredible. Now say it," she snaps.

He does know what he is meant to say. It is a confession, a conclusion, a revelation.

The curse of enlightenment. Sublime self-knowledge.

"Fuck off," he says.

He attempts to spit at her. As his actions so often are, the act is ill-intended, worse executed, and heedlessly self-defeating.

The globule of spittle hangs off the end of his chin. It flaps in the wind like so many hateful tirades as he says:

"Let me wake up. Now. I'll do the right thing. I'll change."

"Much too late for that, don't you think? You've been trained on Dickens, I'm afraid. There is no redemption being offered here."

His eyes bug out of his warty sockets. Perhaps for the first time, he feels something approximating fear. Not the burning, lacerating, familiar, angry fear of humiliation; for the first time, he fears for his own survival, feels the desperation of true helplessness, of being on the receiving end of another's complete and utter antipathy.

He tries again to cry out, for security, who are always posted outside the door; they will come running, wake him up, restore the rightful order, make bedtime great again.

This time, he does manage to scream, but not for his own taste of small suffering.

As his mouth hangs open against his will, against every attempt to close, ignore, silence it, his screams are the cries of the children pulled from their mother's arms, who are bleeding of his bombs, who are starving of his aid denied; of the mother who muffles sobs with a pillow because she has gone without so that her children may have, the desperate fathers howling after the child swept away by flood, the despondent elder dying slowly and painfully without care.

The malicious, foaming, frothing cheers of his supporters and sycophants.

"Well, I'll admit, my gag reflex would appreciate your leaving my sight," the Crone says as she waves away his breath, "But then again, you've never really been bothered about your repugnance. You rather revel in it, I should say. Made your emptiness the whole world's problem, didn't you? Go on then, shoo, wake up, you dirty rotten bleeder," the she says, clapping her hands together as close as she can possibly get to his face without actually touching him.

No need to be catching anything on the way out.

ARIA FOR A GRASSHOPPER

***

His last unconscious thoughts are the vague sense of unearned triumph he has carried within him his whole life, of the world being set to rights.

...And that her clap sounded suspiciously like the last blow of an axe before a tree trunk breaks, falls, bites the dust.

In the instant before he opens his eyes, he renews his lifelong vow — his calling, really — to take the rest of the forest down with him.

***

The old man wakes with a start.

He thrashes around in his bedclothes, tangling stringy limbs with satin sheets — hot pink, his favorite color, which shines even in the darkness, serves as a beacon to call him back to his waking realm.

He has heard security whispering around corners about his fondness for the soft and the neon, a bedroom fit for an over-privileged preadolescent girl. He knows they all suppress their sniggers at the twisted toenails, corns, and calluses they assist in stuffing into his shoes every morning. At the occasional lapse in continence.

In the morning, he will have them all fired, finally — security, secretaries, staffers, servants. All of them drunk, worthless losers who can't keep their noses out of each other's business or blow. He has a country to run, a world to dominate, aches to assuage, and cravings to satiate.

Dissidents to punish.

If anything, this nightmare has taught him to live even more in the here and now. Never miss an opportunity, even at, what time is it? — 2:48 AM. He'll fire those fuckers now, call in the generals, wage a new war somewhere, domestic, abroad, online.

He'll sleep soundly to the symphony of their suffering, lit large on the seventy-inch scrolling screen on his wall, chirons flashing his name again, and again, and again.

The stuff of dreams.

His toenails scrape the silk sheets as he disentangles himself from his bedding. With effort, he sits up inelegantly, wiggles his crooked feet until they meet the stability of the fine wool shag carpet, wriggles them free as the fibers stick to the dry, peeling skin on his heels and bunions, clinging to him like reaching root balls. Some of them disengage, attach to his feet, trailing him as he shuffles to the bathroom, all the while reaching to plant themselves in one spot, to take hold, worm their way back into the fabric of being.

He makes his way to the toilet, lowers his neon silk pajama bottoms, and fidgets himself onto the seat. Best get comfortable, he thinks, as his entrails gurgle.

Gonna be here a while.

He strains ineffectually, all the while the fibrous roots which have claimed his feet are slithering into the floor tiles, forming an impossible, unbreakable union between marble and wool.

He gives one last good push, concedes to the inevitable victory of his chronic constipation. So much winning everywhere, gotta lose somewhere, may as well be his own guts, goddamn doctors poking and prodding, asking him about diet and fiber intake, he had ripped the goddamn pressure cuff off, threw it in their smug faces, mother and father both lived to a ripe old age, eating, drinking, and smoking as they pleased.

He stands, bends to pull up his pajama pants.

Pick up the pants, pick up the phone, get the heads to rolling, he thinks, in the characteristically sing-songy way his internal monologue has labored on since childhood.

He hums a little ditty in happy anticipation.

He takes a small step forward to better balance, finds himself bolted to the ground. The wool carpet filaments have fully rooted into the marble, requiring only brief contact with a relic of the natural world for the spell to take hold.

The ties that bind.

His heart, already under considerable strain from a lifetime of both abuse and unregenerate lack of use, careens to an unaccustomed pace in his panic.

He falls face first, pants down, onto the marble floor.

The impact on his left anterior descending artery lets loose plaque which has been lying in wait for decades.

It detaches itself almost entirely from the arterial wall, forming a clever, valve-like apparatus which perfectly plugs the artery, ceasing blood flow to the authoritarian's heart.

It is 3 A.M.

If only he had his phone, he could implore his faithful. If only he could shout to the guards outside, who will undoubtedly find him bare-assed, balls clinging to his leg like soggy prunes, cheek melted to the floor, mouth open like a dead catfish.

They'll pass the pictures secretly amongst themselves, snorting like hyenas until one of his staunchest staff puts a stop to it, all the while plotting their next moves, whispering behind doors, plodding, conspiring, colluding.

Then, the vultures will descend.

***

An old woman stands outside a palace. Her hands grip the iron bars of the barrier fence.

Her knuckles are pale with the seizing tension. In the moonlight, her skin appears as glinting ripples on a lake, gentle, concentric waves begetting waves.

Each crease is an achievement, a consummation, and she has so, so very many.

She wears bermuda shorts, and a t-shirt which has been altered such that it exposes one of her knobby shoulders.

Her t-shirt reads: "1st Annual Lake Lanier Cardboard Boat Regatta — Come One, Come All! Who Will Triumph and Who Will Fall?"

She watches the palace intently, breaks her gaze only to crouch periodically away from the roaming spotlight, which shines through the razor wire atop the barrier fence like crystallized lightning.

Never losing her grip.

The windows of the palace are dark. *They must have all passed out early tonight*, she thinks.

ARIA FOR A GRASSHOPPER

Even from this distance, even with her ancient eyes, she can make out the details of the palatial architecture, such as it is.

A hodgepodge of Old World styles simulated in cheap modern materials — where gargoyles should be carved of granite, they are molded plastic sprayed with pebble-paint; where buttresses should be flying from the hands of trans-generational masons, they support nothing, plywood shells only; where angels should be sculpted by skilled hands, eyes rolled up to heaven, they are plaster facsimiles with molting faces.

Like they circumvented designers, architects, and artisans entirely and went straight for the Halloween warehouse mega-store.

The Crone rolls her eyes on behalf of the sightless angels. Least she can do, poor things.

She stands there, keeping vigil, until some hours later, lights begin illuminating the windows.

It begins with a corner window on the third floor. Then, several more, room by room, floor by floor, until the entire palace is illuminated from within.

When black, windowless vehicles begin swarming the compound, she has all the confirmation she needs.

Before she releases the iron bars, she surveys the back of her hand. A pretty little wave has formed on her littlest finger, deep and ornate, a crowning jewel.

She smiles, turning her grip this way and that, studying it like a bride-to-be.

Very pleased indeed.

She releases her grip, wriggling her fingers against her palms to warm them up, to stimulate circulation.

She feels the distinct coarseness of wet, crumbling rust, which has bonded with her palms during their communion with the iron fence.

Funny, she thinks, *seemed solid before.*

Heterogenous solutions — notoriously unpredictable things, she has learned from experience.

She wipes her hands clean on her bermuda shorts. She has already missed her *Wings* reruns, and *The Honeymooners* besides, but this... this was truly must-see.

The rust stains shine like twin pools of blood in the dawn.

***

Months later, rumors begin trickling out of the palace.

It seems in the very spot — which spot? — a tree has sprouted from a slab of marble.

Indigenous to the region, the tree continues to grow at an exponential — unnatural, say the whispers — rate.

Despite all efforts at extermination, it is due to punch its way out of the roof, walls, and windows of the third floor.

They say it will bring about a precipitous and fatal decline in the palace's infrastructure.

Come on in, it will say to its sister seeds and saplings, *this has always been ours.*

ARIA FOR A GRASSHOPPER

Recollection

It's the weather that does it.

The loosening of the leaves

as they trade

an old life

for a radiant after —

No longer able to bargain with

the softening of the sun,

the rank flagrancy

of dormant grass

and wet soil

smeared on your hands

as you collect totems

of stone

from the earth that is

ARIA FOR A GRASSHOPPER

yours but no longer —

Two tries to get it out of your

system,

to

rewire

the

neurons

but —

the earth's tilt,

she insists —

your hippocampus activates

when the leaves smell like

childhood scrapes

and clod

and clay

and tears

and the breeze is a

symphony

of memories

whispered.

How is a body to move

forward

when the season remakes

itself

as you

relapse —

fall

into the gap,

the pain point's inception,

on a day

so beautiful

the air affirms your lungs

ARIA FOR A GRASSHOPPER

by being?

Is this the curse

of delight?

Oh, to be free

of the softness

of me.

V. Destruction

"While men have chosen the ravages of ruination-"

The Eye

There is a great eye.

It endures at its own pleasure, somewhere between existence and the place beyond it. Because The Eye has no purpose beyond persistence, no stake in anything at all, really, it rolls up and about and around at will.

The Eye has meandered in this manner for as long as there has been anything to regard, though it remembers a dark, unhappy time when there was only the singularity to see: an infinitely dense, infinitesimal point in space to look.

This was an especially boring and discouraging time to be an incorporeal entity whose only power is observation, as infinitely dense singularities didn't do much in those days.

Nothing, but untapped potential.

The Eye's patience, of course, was rewarded in spectacular fashion, and the wonders have since never ceased. If it could speak, it would certainly say that the wonders have never ceased, if there were anyone worth telling.

Sometimes, the Eye rolls itself back and tries to picture what the nothingness surrounding the singularity looked like. It cannot recall, try as it might, though it does not allow itself to become too discouraged, too mired in past disappointments.

Nowadays, there are so many things to look upon, and only forever to do so.

***

The Eye rolls lazily in the direction of a nebula it has been monitoring, which has devoted itself to the violent process of forming a coupling of new stars.

The Eye has seen this process play itself out billions of times, but, being enlightened, it does feel that one should appreciate the little things.

The Eye scans in the direction of a supernova which has been active as of late. No real change, except the destruction of some habitable and inhabited planets, which have had the misfortune of crossing paths with the supernova's gamma ray bursts.

Lately, the Eye has found that celestial cataclysm fails to hold its interest for very long. The Eye is aware of a looming, leering black hole that will devour the nebula before the coupling of stars has a chance to become anything worth watching.

The supernova will continue to radiate outward; the black hole will bend time.

The physics of the predictable.

ARIA FOR A GRASSHOPPER

Lately, the Eye has found itself much more interested in the minutiae of less-predictable living things. It is interested in forming a hypothesis — perhaps even a presiding theory — about the infinitesimally small nature of life. Life, a singularity of its own, with all its confined possibilities — the unaccountability of beings who think themselves conscious, significant, unexpendable.

The Eye seeks to see it all clearly, unobstructed by the astigmatism of sentiment.

Retinal detachment, it thinks.

It looks around for someone to exchange a knowing glance, a fellow omniscient sentience who appreciates wordplay and the eternal silliness inherent in everything.

There is no visual cue, no signal.

The Eye flutters.

***

The Eye sweeps in the direction of a favorite planet which, historically, has teemed with life.

It trains its focus.

A black cat crosses a road.

The Eye wonders, until it sees that the cat has been tracking a weakened baby snake, who will disappear into a wormhole and starve as The Eye observes.

The cat lays nearby, watching, not out of need, but out of boredom. It is springtime.

The cat will nap in the comfort of a sunbeam and saunter away some hours later, having forgotten about the baby snake entirely, all things being in abundance — light, comfort, water, respite. Satiety.

The Eye will watch this same black cat collapse in the inescapable heat of summer, its tongue dropped stupidly out of its open mouth. It will blow up like a balloon in a department-store Christmas parade as it is devoured by carrion bacteria.

It will watch as the cat's putrefied remains are peeled from the asphalt, placed in a boiling pot, and rendered into chunks of viscera and lard which are greedily eaten by a small group of scorched, grabbing, desperate creatures.

The Eye watches as one of the creatures sneaks a bone from the pot, begins sucking the miserly marrow, while the others, back turned, are licking their fingers, searching with dry tongues for the morsel, the bit, the molecule, which will reverse their own bodies' consumption of itself.

A mouthful, a reverie, a delusion.

The Eye regards as the other creatures see the bone-sucker, nothing more than a temporarily sentient skeleton itself, attempting to mine public calories for private gain.

They will enclose him in a rage. In the act of murder, their bodies will metabolize the smattering of nutrients the cat has provided. Waste not, want not.

They will render bone-sucker in the same pot as the cat.

The Eye chooses to avert itself at this time.

No need to tend to foregone conclusions.

ARIA FOR A GRASSHOPPER

***

A former flower bed burns in the same sun that has killed legions of crops on this planet, a process exacerbated by a factor obscured from the watcher.

The former flower bed was one of many like it at this location, sharing its seeds with fountains, shifting its fragrance into the nose of many a distinguished guest, permitting petals in the wind to be carried out to sea, bypassing the sea's stunted compatriot: the regulation-sized saltwater pool, which sits crumbling into dust.

The Eye knows about gases, knows heat the likes of which this planet can only speculate upon, throw numbers at, but cannot for its own existence understand why everything on this planet is being so dramatic about a few extra billion tons of gas, an absurdly miniscule shift in heat energy.

A planetary lacking in perspective.

Place all the universe's troubles on a table, and inevitably, this planet would choose its own, The Eye thinks.

The Eye chews over — not for the first time — life's inability to thrive without the existence of other life, a confounding phenomena it refuses to accept as reality, so antithetical it is to its own subsistence, which depends on nothing except its own will.

Everything is. Everything is as it wants it to be.

***

The Eye scrolls its gaze beneath the former flower bed, where is located a favorite scene of late, a tableau with which The Eye can truly identify: an observing visionary.

Here, a billionaire stretches his body out beside a pool of water, in a habitat he has had made to replicate his former domain on the surface.

This cross-section of earth is infinitely pleasing to The Eye, as the billionaire has seen to it that each detail of the scorched garden above has been aligned precisely, within fractions of a millimeter, with its replicant below.

But for a few feet of crust and dirt, but for the better part of a decade, one might have viewed the cross section of this land and seen only a horizontal reflection.

As above, so below.

To The Eye, this thwarted symmetry is singularly affecting. To The Eye, the reproduction of living things with immortal copies makes only logical sense.

To The Eye, the billionaire saw the inevitable, resisted. A far-sighted prognosticator.

If The Eye could feel kinship, it might have admitted a fondness for the billionaire.

***

The billionaire yawns and feels the familiar bubbling in his guts that indicates his need to feed.

The Eye watches as the billionaire pushes a button on the arm of his chair.

Another person materializes, dressed all in white.

This person appears much more haggard than the billionaire, despite the clean, crisp uniform, despite the freshness of his haircut, the perfection of his fingernails.

The Eye has come to associate this hollow-eyed appearance with "suffering," a word it observes frequently used on this planet, in many of its languages.

The Eye notes, not for the first time, no such mark of suffering on the billionaire's face.

"Yes, sir?" the person in white says. His voice cracks as he says "sir."

"I keep telling you, call me Noah," the billionaire says, reclined in his lounge chair. He does not move or remove his sunglasses to make eye contact with the person in white.

"I'm sorry — Noah," the person in white says. "What can I do for you?"

"How about you make us some lunch?" the billionaire asks.

"What would you like?" the person in white asks.

"Oh, I don't know. What do we have?" The billionaire pauses. "And don't tell me it's only the goddamn rations Jerry had flown in. You said the hydroponics were doing well. Produce any day now. I'd kill for something goddamn fresh. Something that doesn't turn to goddamn mush the second I put it in my mouth."

"I'm doing my best, sir," the person in white says.

The Eye clocks that his cheeks have flushed.

"It's not you," the billionaire says, sighing. "Though the last one could have made chicken salad out of chicken shit. And I do mean that fairly literally."

The Eye sees a nearly imperceptible change on the person in white's face. A flash of something — resentment. Violence.

These moments, this is why the Eye watches. These data sets chip away at the eternal mystery, helps it see more clearly.

The person in white bites his lip, hard. The Eye notes this gesture, wonders at its purpose.

"Ah, well," the billionaire says ruefully. "Plague'll do that. Kill off talent," he waves his hand, -indiscriminately. "But man, the things he could do with government cheese. Almost made me feel like I was back on holiday in France, before all this-."

The billionaire sweeps his hand again at nothing and no one.

The billionaire sits up on his lounge chair and finally turns his body towards the person in white, who is standing mute, arms behind his back.

The billionaire removes his sunglasses, squints uncomfortably, pushes a button on the arm of his chair. The electric lighting changes from a imitation of late afternoon to an effigy of dusk.

Synthetic crickets begin to sing a symphony through speakers that are carefully hidden throughout the landscaping, in every room of the billionaire's underground dwelling.

The billionaire focuses his gaze on the person in white. His eyes become slits.

"You're not re-thinking our arrangement, are you?" he asks.

Panic flashes on the person in white's face. This is plainly visible both to the Eye and to the billionaire.

"No, of course not," the person in white says.

The Eye doesn't understand tone, or subtext, takes all it sees at face value, takes the person in white's word for it.

Here, we have a mutually beneficial working relationship. Here is a man with much to give, serving a man with less.

The universal constant: the exchange of energy.

The billionaire straightens himself up. He stares at the person in white long enough that the person in white begins to shift from foot to foot.

"I will do my best to get the hydroponics producing," he says. "It's just — I don't know. I'm doing everything correctly, but the plants just wither. I can't explain it. I'm not a botanist —"

"Don't tell me you weren't growing pot indoors at whatever culinary institute you stumbled out of. Besides, there's the books. We have the instruction manuals from the team. My team. The best team. It's not goddamn rocket science, it's tomatoes. It's fucking... I don't know, squash."

The billionaire tilts his head, studies the man in white as if observing he were in the company of another human for the first time. The billionaire allows his shoulders to slump.

"Jerry tells me he's having the same problem, truth be told. We'll have to check the systems. Air quality, maybe."

The billionaire reclines again in his chair, pushes yet another button. The sound of ocean waves begins echoing through the chamber.

The volume overwhelms what is, all things considered to The Eye, an immensely small space on an immensely small planet in what is increasingly a small universe.

Yet, these humans posture at their own expansiveness.

"Have I ever told you where my wife is?" the billionaire asks, raising his voice over the artificial waves. The recording mimics a calm tide on a tropical beach; he has chosen this in lieu of "incoming storm on Atlantic shores," and some other simulations he finds too overstimulating, too reminiscent of flooding prime shorefront property, screams drowned by tsunami.

Sinking stocks, sinking yachts.

The person in white relaxes his shoulders, dares roll his own eyes.

Of course he knows where she is, the whole (remaining) world knows. The timeless story of Shitty Helen of Troy. Severed friendship. Carved up domains. Castes. Needless death.

The senselessness of the suffering, the billions worth nothing.

Never justice. Not on any scale worth weighing.

"Left me for someone else, a friend. Bigger bunker. Hit a man right where it hurts," the billionaire says, fist to chest.

"And the kids. Spoiled brats are off in the settlements. Say they can't rot away down here. They want to *help*."

The billionaire makes a twin gesture with the first two fingers on both hands.

"*This* is helping, I said. Continuing the species. Underground farming. Carbon capture — when I had a team, when I have one again. What more could they want? What more could they ask? I should go up there and wither away as a martyr? We're saving the fucking world down here. We are the innovator class."

The person in white swallows hard, says nothing.

ARIA FOR A GRASSHOPPER

The billionaire slams his fist on the arm of his chair. The weather in the room becomes erratic, flashing from night to day, season to season, calm to storm.

The person in white closes his eyes, steadies himself with a hand on the wall.

The Eye sees the person in white putting a hand over his heart, as if that contact could have some sort of effect on the physical systems contained therein.

The Eye thinks hard, struggling to form a conclusion which has been threatening to materialize for some time now. The Eye is aware that this species contains layers upon layers of fleshy mechanism, as do many species it has observed. A man can build a refuge under the earth, harness energy in wires and funnel gas through tubes. He can ensnare the sound of the sea, shine sunlight through bulbs, harvest every drop of moisture within the radius of his empire — and yet, no man has ever achieved the ability to reach into his own chest, poke through a few inches of flesh, and repair himself.

The billionaire growls at the misfiring technology, slams a button on his control panel, over and over again, until his hair has grown unruly and his sunglasses — once a status symbol, now, blinders — have fallen victim to his breaking fists.

The electric sun rises until it is once again afternoon in the bunker.

The billionaire breathes heavily. Sitting sideways on his lounge chair, he runs his fingers through his hair in an attempt to set it to rights. To keep up appearances.

The billionaire and the man in white stare at each other.

The Eye cannot interpret what is exchanged in this look, the information inscrutable to the naked eye.

"I'll have that imitation tuna again, I guess," the billionaire says. "Just try to do something interesting with it this time."

***

The Eye grows bored with talk of tuna, revolves itself inward to access memory: a favorite settlement.

In the past, The Eye had taken a special interest in this place, but like a discarded toy, its amusements have been all but forgotten.

The Eye finds itself worrying at a piece of information, like squeezing a splinter until it bursts from under the skin:

The billionaire indeed had children who had taken what resources they could from him, what the billionaire was unable to prevent them from taking, and set off for the settlements.

To help, they claimed. To fry like shit in the sun, the billionaire countered.

The billionaire's reference to "Jerry," had fired some dormant neurons in The Eye, and while The Eye didn't know what a "Jerry" was, it recalled there being a "Jerry" domain near this particular settlement.

Everything was "Jerry" as far as The Eye could see.

***

The Eye is aware that humans, in a time before, would connect reels of images together. The reels were played for their amusement by projecting light through pictures, a living memory.

Lens to lens, dust to dust.

Some of these images were meant to be frightening, entertainment induced by evoking the most visceral, upsetting emotions in the viewer.

The Eye supposes it does the same with the images that it has gathered, though the emotional investment — this, it cannot understand.

These images are, then they were, then strung together in an attempt to make meaning.

To The Eye, the meaning is the witnessing.

***

The Eye recalls a conversation it observed in this settlement some time prior — months, years, maybe.

The Eye begins summoning stacks of images, flicking them left to right, assembling, projecting them across its optic nerve, for the first time in its existence, storytelling:

A young woman stands in a warehouse, the details of which have evaporated from The Eye's peripherals.

Her hair is pulled back, loose, dry, as if a single static shock would set it afire.

Her chin is raised, as is her right eyebrow, and her mouth is tightly drawn. Her skin is red and angry; a flake of dry skin escapes her shoulder like so many mythical snowflakes.

Her eyes are wet and alert, boring into her companion's.

The Eye had tuned in belatedly, missed the exposition. It was caught up for weeks watching an earthworm wriggle, cease, dry, crumble, fly.

The man, whose hollow cheeks and firm brow nonetheless betray a softness The Eye cannot quantify, looks back at the woman with dark, glittering eyes.

The Eye also knows this word: "affection," and is glad finally to be able to use it in the correct context.

"Say that again, I dare you," the young woman says.

The man takes the young woman's face in his hands.

"What," he says, pauses, "am I supposed to do with this?"

The young woman pulls the man's hands off her face.

"You do recall," she says, "the effort that went into obtaining it? The planning?"

"I do-" he begins.

"And then you will also recall," she says, "your consenting to said plan?"

"I never said-"

"Don't. Don't you dare."

"I thought you did dare me."

The man smiles wide, playfully. The young woman's defenses drop temporarily; she suppresses a smirk. They pause for a minute, surveying each other, deciding where to land the next blow, whether to make it glancing or direct, whether to aim for the soft stuff.

She speaks first, as she always has. It is what he has come to love about her.

"I went. All the way there. The team scrounged up the gas, they bypassed Jerry's security. I had to drive for hours, avoid the hostile settlements, watch for roamers. Sleep with a gun. Goddamn near fried like shit in the sun."

"You're glowing. Like you just got back from holiday."

"I had to knock on his goddamn blast door, like a guest." Now, she is yelling.

"All things being fair, you were a guest."

His ability to be entirely unserious in the most dire of circumstances is what she has come to love about him. Sometimes.

"I had to speak to — him. I had to pretend I was there to stay, that I was sorry, that I was wrong. I had to convince the chef to go along with it, to agree to die probably having never eaten another green thing in his life- ."

"Death by Chef Boyardee."

"He could die down there, with Dad. They'll starve. I had to correct his notion that Jerry's rations are inexhaustible. That was tough for him to accept. Keeping Dad in the dark, keeping him down there until it's over... he's making an incredible sacrifice."

"Aren't we all?"

She falls into his arms, and he leans his head on hers.

Her voice is muffled, "Yes, now I need you to *do* something with it, you obnoxious fuck."

"I wasn't there when the tech was developed. He had fired me by then. I don't have-"

His voice is quivering. The Eye tries to put a pin on the emotional expression in his eyes, in the tremor of his mouth — contrition, maybe. Weakness, yes.

She looks up at him with the widest eyes he had ever known to exist.

He relents.

"-It'll take me a while. And, I'm gonna need some help."

He looks at her pointedly.

She is weeping now.

Strange, The Eye thinks. Weeping is for unfulfilled wants, for despair. For rinsing the dust from one's cornea.

"I never did finish my degree," she says.

"You never had the chance. Top of your class, though. You're an excellent candidate," he says formally, "Too bad about the societal collapse."

"This tech... it could feed a lot of people. It could begin-"

"I know."

"And I essentially killed my father for it."

"*Comme ci, comme ça.*"

The young woman starts laughing with her whole chest, her shoulders shaking.

"He's gonna be... so mad at me."

The man laughs. Their laughter echoes off the walls of the warehouse.

Outside, a motley group of people stands eavesdropping.

The Eye regards them with disgust. Why listen to what one cannot see?

At the sound of the couple's laughter, the group visibly relaxes.

It will be done, they say, wordlessly with their many sets of eyes.

"How is Noah? I trust he's well," the man asks, wiping tears from his eyes with grubby fingers.

The man lifts his hand from his face. Both of them stare at the droplet which has formed on the tip of his index.

He extends his finger to her.

She opens her mouth, and with the flick of his forefinger, he drops it in.

The woman shakes her head. Her eyes flutter.

"He was just happy to have someone to play pickleball with. First thing he said when he opened the door — opened the door himself, no less- is that the chef is horseshit, and he hopes I had a good time out there with the scavengers and cannibals. He won't notice the tech is missing until it's too late, if ever. Probably still standing there with his paddle, waiting. No way he won't notice everything else I took this time, though."

She grins.

"Whole truckload of General Jerry's finest. Coolants, canned cheese, water harvester. Spare parts. All the freeze-dried vegetables you can dream about."

"Did he ask about your sister?"

"No. He asked about Mom and Jerry, though."

"And what did you tell him?"

"Wedded bliss. Jerry's got the biggest bunker, the best bunker. Magnificent chef. Fertile territory. Acres of underground farmland."

"Why the lies? The truth is so much... worse."

"When has he ever been moved by the truth?"

"God, I'd have killed to see his face."

"Well, in a way, I guess that's what I did."

***

The Eye had tuned out at that moment. Small talk is for small ears, smaller minds. It had allowed itself to become distracted by a fly buzzing erratically by, in search of a nitrogen-rich landing pad. It could have sworn it saw the fly's wings disintegrate mid-flight, its cuticles shimmering, then shattering into bits in the sun.

Or maybe it was a trick of the light.

***

The Eye struggles to locate Jerry's domain. It searches near the remembered settlement, around it. Up, down, over, across acres and miles and millenia.

Vanished.

An infuriating failure, an unaccustomed defect in its perfect sight, its unfettered scope.

The Eye feels itself lose control. It rolls, shakes, quivers, nearly blinds itself with rage. It lapses into unconscious lucidity, unable to control the images flashing in front of itself, but actively participating in them.

The Eye is a cat, then it is a dying snake hooked on his claw. The Eye is the ashes of a wildfire. The Eye is trapped in a tube of fluorescent coolant. A thirsty child. A sobbing mother.

The Eye is palsied. Paralyzed.

When it regains a semblance of muscular control, it rolls up into itself for an indeterminate amount of time.

ARIA FOR A GRASSHOPPER

Wake me if I fall asleep, it says, to no one at all.

***

The Eye comes to.

It does not know how long it has been out of commission, but it is grateful for the time it has taken to rebalance, align once more with its intuition, its sense of its place in the cosmic scheme.

The Eye blinks and trains its focus on its pet planet.

It sees that it remains much as before. Brown. Pockets of green near the poles that expand when hemispherically turned away from the sun.

Massive storms, small sectors of lights at night.

Telltale formations indicating underground dwellings. More of them, bigger.

***

The Eye scans for something of interest. Some sign of life it doesn't have to look too deeply to see. Mercifully, it does not have to strain.

The Eye is caught by two beings huddled in an isolated corner, in a crumbling building, surrounded by arid decay. It peers closer.

The beings are covered in rags, all their belongings piled on the floor next to them.

They are thin, impossibly so. Living skeletons.

The intensity of their gazes — The Eye cannot meet them.

This is a new problem for The Eye. It has never, in all of existence, looked away from anything.

The Child sprawls on the floor, attempting to trade some of his heat with the floor, to find some relief.

The Mother stares despondently into the distance.

The Eye focuses, refocuses, zooms in as close as it can get to the mother's cheek. Under its microscope, the Eye notes an irregular pattern in the mother's skin cells, a nuclear disorganization. Nothing interesting about that, it thinks. It zooms out two clicks, to the surface, notes the weeping, bleeding sore on her face where the irregular cells reside.

But the Mother isn't thinking about the cancer. For the first time since he was born, she's not even thinking about the boy, has moved him entirely from her consciousness, a reprieve from the horror, a blotting out in her mind's eye.

She is thinking about a pool party from a long time ago. The abundance. The coolers and coolers of popsicles, the cotton candy machine, the balloon animals. A whole-ass petting zoo.

An absent father. A distracted mother.

She is thinking about when the gardener noticed the party needed a boost, despite there being available everything a kid could want: Just Ask, the family crest.

Until the question was, "Play with us?" Until the question was, "Can't you make it this time?" Until the question was, "Take us with you?"

The partygoers, invited out of obligation, rather than want — "Well who the hell else would you two want at this thing anyway?" — were all sitting in various configurations, spread out cliques planted throughout the gargantuan garden.

The gardener had been watering one of the many identical flower beds.

She and her sister were petting the pony.

The softest thing she had ever felt, until she had stroked her baby boy's head.

The boy — *no, not now*, she thinks.

She looked up, caught the gardener looking at her with that face some grownups sometimes had: *I feel sorry for you. I really do. Even here, even now.*

He winked and smiled.

"Whoops!" he said, as he lifted the hose, spraying a group of girls who had looked for the duration of the party as if they had smelled something unpleasant.

All the world in the palm of his hand, and he still couldn't make you cool, she thinks.

The girls had shrieked, run away, scattered to various shelters around the garden grounds.

"I don't know what's going on!" the gardener yelled. "It's like my arm has a mind of its own!"

He began spraying the partygoers, whose shrieks and giggles were enough to pique the grownups' interest.

Her mother, looking up from her phone, out and over her pinot grigio, fire in her eyes at the commotion, the attention he was drawing to himself. All eyes on the gardener.

One of the popular girls decided to put an end to this nonsense. She marched over to the gardener, wrestled the hose out of his "resisting" hand, sprayed him until he was soaked, arms out, laughing.

What began as a power play ending in... something else. Something like shared humanity.

Water has that effect, she thinks: *in abundance, in shortage, in absentia.*

At that moment, she chose to be bold. She signaled with her eyes to her sister to leave the pony, we have a mission.

She strode into the middle of the fray between the popular girl and the gardener, opened her arms wide, ready to be sprayed.

At the time, it didn't seem like a baptism.

The popular girl, still laughing, made eye contact with her, really saw her, she thinks, though maybe hindsight is only magical thinking. Illusory.

The popular girl handed her the hose. A peace offering. Detente.

She smiled and sprayed the popular girl. Then, everyone.

The next few hours remain some of the happiest of her childhood.

The suggestion of an impromptu sleepover. The whispered secrets. The popcorn.

The belonging.

Until Mom's pinot hangover kicked in. Until she slipped on the wet tile. Until someone looking for a bathroom opened the wrong door, saw what they shouldn't.

Until the gardener wasn't seen on the grounds again.

***

"Don't fall asleep, my love," the mother says.

"Why?" the Child asks. "I can have sleep for dinner."

They have done this journey many times before, she thinks, and yet, they have wandered so far off course, so far from the friendly settlements.

Dust storm, scrambled signal, desperation.

"I want you to have some water first," the Mother says.

"We have water?" the Child says.

"I've been saving it for you."

The Child lifts his head to look at his mother. She attempts a smile.

This moment, she knows they won't survive. Not until the rains, not until they are deemed gone too long. Not until a search party can track them, tracing her markers, if they can find them buried in dust, to here.

The Child raises an eyebrow.

"What's going on?" the Child asks. Not asks, tells — he has seen for some time. He has allowed her to reach her own conclusion.

"I-" the Mother starts. "I have a nice meal for you. And a full canteen."

The Mother's voice breaks despite this excellent news.

The Eye blinks in confusion.

The Child uses every ounce of remaining energy he has to crawl to his mother.

He curls up on her lap. She rests her dirty face on his head, draws him closer despite the heat.

She begins humming. A lullaby, an aria, a hymn. A plea.

The little boy buries his face in her chest as she holds him to her stomach.

She rubs his back and pats his bottom, her baby, her heart beating outside her body.

"Mama? Can I have it now?" he whispers.

She doesn't respond.

"Please, Mama?"

The mother reaches into her shirt and pulls out a small paper packet. A tiny square, which has cost her dearly to procure, to protect. An infinitely dense weight on her heart. A price she'd have paid a million times over.

She unfolds the packet, hands shaking.

"Are you sure?"

The boy looks at her. The Eye cannot see, cannot understand the information that is passed between their eyes. It is immeasurable, unquantifiable.

He opens his mouth.

"Close your eyes, now," she says.

"Save some for you too, Mama."

The Mother swallows hard, pours the entirety of the powder into her son's mouth. There was only ever enough for one. She refuses to allow him to suffer. She will bear it.

"I love you, more than anything."

"I love you more."

"No, I love you more."

A game, which she has always been happy to lose.

"Ok. You can win this time."

"Mama, will you tell me how it was?"

"No," she says, "I will tell you how it's going to be."

***

When his breathing stops, he appears at peace.

She is transported in her mind's eye back to a comfortable room, filled with colors and textures she hasn't seen in years. Pastels, softness, plenty.

Illusions, all.

She croons her baby's name while he sleeps in her arms.

He smiles big, toothless, unconscious of the connection between those sounds and their meaning, conscious only of the comfort he feels, the familiarity of the notes of her voice, the smell of her milk, the primal protection she offers.

The bonding of their atoms.

The cataclysm of their splitting.

***

She used to wish, sometimes, that she could reverse time.

Not in the way her parents mumbled banal platitudes — *time is a thief,* they'd say in public, as they pulled on her and her sister's hair, or pressed down hard on their shoulders to assist in the illusion of familial bliss.

Later, they'd be punished for their grimaces.

No. She'd wish she could reverse time, put him back in her womb. Play the old film backwards — the ovum that was him would fly back up her fallopian, the successful sperm cell would rewind itself back and out. From whence it came.

Keep going, keep rewinding, and she'd never have existed at all either.

The only surefire prophylactic for suffering.

But the boy, she'd think, willed himself into existence. His life mattered.

Inspired her to go, every time, even when she didn't want to, didn't think she had the strength, on their missions, to scope out other settlements. To form bonds.

Inspired the leaders to let their guards down, when they'd look into the biggest eyes she had ever known to exist.

When he'd say, "We just want to share."

Wore her down enough to say "Yes," when he'd ask "Will you take me too?"

Everyone knowing very well it could be the last time.

Convinced her sister to see their father again, for the good of all. And that mission is bearing fruit, in every sense.

She said she couldn't look him in the eye again if she hadn't gone. She had always loved him as her own, but then again, so did they all.

***

She isn't at peace.

She knows their disappearance will cause immeasurable suffering in the settlement.

She knows her sister will never stop looking for them, stop asking about a pair matching their description. The next settlement, maybe. Further North. Deeper underground. It will be an ache without remedy.

She wishes she could live to see the harvest. To see her boy taste a peach, bite into a slice of watermelon. To see his cheeks turn pink with the sticky pulp. He doesn't know what he doesn't know.

She isn't at peace, but she has come to a resolution. They have done what they could.

It is all anyone can do.

***

The Eye will watch as the Mother stays here, hours, maybe days, waiting for her breath to cease, willing her heart to stop. To know nothing.

He's gone he's gone he's gone please take me too.

The Eye will watch as the Mother finally fades, until the fleshy mechanism in her chest– which has nevertheless persisted in moving a dwindling amount of nutrients, oxygen, hope, through her body — catches up to the rest of her, realizes it is irreparably broken.

The Eye will linger, looking for them both, knowing perfectly well their bodies are right there, don't be ridiculous.

Still, The Eye looks. It feels something like — longing? Desperation. The terror of the misplaced. A holy absence.

It scans the atmosphere that surrounds this planet. It peers through nebulae, into black holes, around the edges of supernovae, mines the depths of dark matter.

It flicks through dimensions, traverses space-time, and yet, it cannot find them.

It struggles to find meaning in witness.

If one can disappear and remain visible simultaneously, what is The Eye supposed to do with that information?

***

The Eye closes. The strain has become too much. It must rest.

If it had a mouth, it might have hummed itself to sleep.

***

Some time later, The Eye opens. It struggles to jettison the accumulated dust from itself, which has solidified into a hunk of space junk in its caruncle.

It attempts to reorient, to wrap itself once more in the fabric of space-time. Now, then:

As ever, it is who. Existence: what.

Where: anywhere it wants to be.

When: a decent place to start.

Why? That is the question indeed.

***

The Eye rolls on toward the nebula it has been monitoring from time to time, the doomed one, naturally. Best to begin comfortably, predictably. Besides, a good judge of how long it has been away will be to measure to what degree the nebula has been consumed by the looming black hole.

ARIA FOR A GRASSHOPPER

Starting small, The Eye thinks. *Mustn't overwhelm the only sense one can rely on.*

The Eye bulges at what it beholds: not an empty, consumed, desolate corner of space-time.

The black hole has arbitrarily averted course away from the nebula. The infant stars persist.

The Eye extrapolates; call it future-sight.

This fertile ground for creation, this nursery, will teem with life.

The Eye resolves to continue its search here, in the not-so-distant hereafter.

***

The Eye yields to fate, allows inertia to take it where it may.

It trains its focus where its gaze falls: the billionaire's bunker.

A group of people are crying. They have wrapped themselves in each other's arms.

At the center of the group is a man and a woman. They too, are crying.

When obstructing heads have moved, when enough of the group has gotten to their knees to kiss the ground, the planters, each other, The Eye sees that the woman is holding a baby.

It sees joy. It sees the baby holding a fat peach, teething at the skin. The baby's grin is wide, exposing two tiny teeth. Her mother kisses her head, holds her lips to it.

Closes her eyes.

It sees years of pain, running in streams down their faces, laughter as deep as the currents of their suffering.

It sees rows upon rows of flowering, green plants.

It sees a man in white, holding a tomato. It sees him, at the others' encouragement, take a bite. It sees the juice run down the corner of his mouth, his tongue flicking out to catch the runoff.

"We have to tell the others," they say.

And The Eye begins to ache. Begins to water. Forms a teardrop.

The Eye visualizes a finger, wills it into existence.

An entire appendage, all for feeling. For doing.

Remarkable.

The Eye wipes the tear from itself. Studies it from all angles. It glistens on its new finger like liquid absolution.

The Eye reaches out and out, turns its finger downward, and with a flick of its new knuckle, drops the tear, filling a lake, moving rivers, trickling into underground streams.

***

A messenger, driving a truck full of produce to the next nearest settlement, head full of knowledge, smiles. He turns on his windshield wipers, wipes a tear from his eye at the beauty of the need.

He rolls the window down and holds his hand out in supplication — no, in thanks — collecting palm after palm of rainwater, letting it trickle down his arm, into the road, and out to commune with untold gallons of its brethren.

It's not the rainy season yet, he thinks, *but, look.*

ARIA FOR A GRASSHOPPER

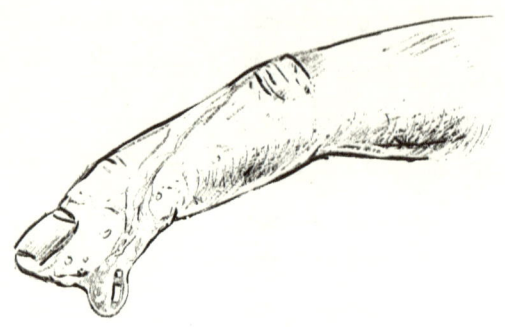

Silence

All is silent —

but nothing is ever really as ever, is it?

There is the ringing in your ears — you know that.

The hum of the cosmic microwave or

maybe just your blood on its way to

its urgent appointment with your recollections.

There is the chirp of a grasshopper in the distance,

resisting, insisting

on being.

There is the croak of

your chuckle,

the catch in

your throat,

the ascendance

ARIA FOR A GRASSHOPPER

of it all —

You know that, too.

There is the friction of the hand you take,

Dunes upon dunes of flesh,

Struggle written on your palms like

fluctuations of the afterglow.

If you align them, just so,

maybe the silence

will compress

into

Creation —

C. G. RENNIE

V. Epilogue- Rebirth

"Mother, with your tears in tow, you will leave the old world behind."

Déjà Vu

It'll happen in a café,

someplace with a reputation for an excellent from-scratch breakfast,

someplace we're both bound to find,

because we always did.

I'll do a double-take for the millionth-and-first time,

because

it can't be.

You'll instinctually turn your head,

white hair floating above worn wingback chair,

brows furrowed over shit-eating grin —

that most paradoxical expression, only yours —

wave me over

as if there's never been a more expected surprise.

You'll pull off your readers,

ARIA FOR A GRASSHOPPER

stick a scrap in your pulpy paperback

grab me hard around the shoulder,

half-standing, half-sitting,

half-real,

and sloppily kiss my cheek.

I'll wish the prickling of your beard permanent,

bite my hand to stop from sobbing.

You'll say, "Now..."

and I'll say, "I know, but..."

the way neither sentence has ever needed to be finished.

I'll hand you the latest wallet-sized picture

missing from your collection,

and you'll give me a bite of your honey-buttered biscuit,

watching, waiting, with

pleasure as my face lights.

"Goddamn, that's good," you'll say, as you take another bite.

I'll tell you about violas and dance solos and accelerated math groups

and you'll admire her picture,

eyes crinkling pride and twinkling delight.

"My Moon," you'll say for the millionth-and-first time

with new meaning.

You'll laugh 'til you wipe your eyes

over the newest hijinks and quotable anecdotes,

announcing your love to the room.

"And how are *you*," you'll say, suddenly, lowering your voice so

that it hovers above scolding.

"You been sleeping?"

You'll raise an eyebrow, tilt your head forward,

all serious concern.

And I'll say, "Mostly. A little."

When you've returned the photograph to your wallet,

slurped the last of your coffee,

ARIA FOR A GRASSHOPPER

I'll know it's time.

You'll slap your knees and say "Welp,"

because the game is on or a project to finish,

a pot to stir or a hill to hike,

tinkering,

puttering,

somewhere

that is not here

with me.

There won't be any bargaining, because there can't be.

When I see you again, and again, and again,

I think it'll go something like this.

C. G. RENNIE

Rebirth

A woman with skin

like waves

watches the edge

of the world.

She stands on the shoreline of yesterday and tomorrow,

examining the macro and

the miniscule

under the microscope of her occluded eye.

Truth:

aye, it is the marrow of

fate

and justice, its

lifeblood.

She will see

her way to

stanching

the bleeding.

When they reject

the reality they have wrought,

when the arc of justice

bends backwards,

she will uncoil

the twisted knots,

hand them the skein of lifetimes, *tsk* her tongue —

disapproval dissolving like

a sacrament —

and say,

"Try again."

Three become one become

three become one again.

ARIA FOR A GRASSHOPPER

Touch the temple

of humankind, oh my loves,

and conjure

Rebirth.

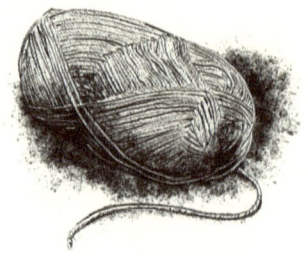

VII. Cri de Cœur

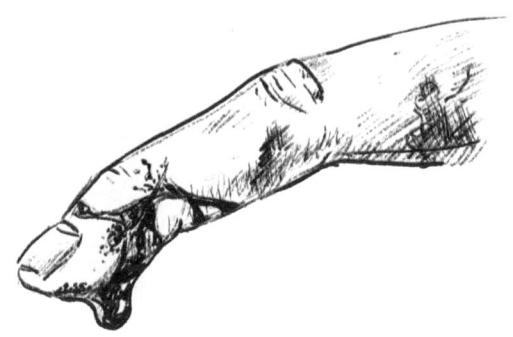

Cri de Cœur

First, there was grief.

Creation grieved to be

the mother of all things.

Mother, you are confined,

Mother, you must free your kind.

While men have chosen the ravages of ruination —

Mother, with your tears in tow, you will leave the old world behind.

Acknowledgements

Thanks, first and foremost, to Brandi Banks, Hannah, and the team at Luminary Publishing House who responded to a very specific question about contest rules on Threads, and were then kind enough to take a chance on reading a few pages. Your support for my vision, my career, and my wellbeing has been incredible, life- and-neurotransmitter-altering, and I will be forever in your debt. Thank you, thank you, thank you.

Thank you to Kevin Falkenberg — whose beautiful art and illustrations grace these pages- but primarily for the life we have built and being the calm keeping me afloat (and laughing) on the stormy seas of my anxieties and pessimism.

Thank you to my daughter, who taught me to love humanity anew and for keeping us on a tight leash since birth.

Thank you to Mom and Colleen, who will understand best.

Thank you to my proverbial villages — friends, family, loved ones lost, friends who are family, the Sisterhood of the Store-Bought Serotonin, dance moms, the Group, the T2C2 nerd crew, the Coffee and Crying Club, the women at Pine City Elementary School who nurtured a precocious reader and writer, students past and present — too many "villagers" to list. Without you, I would cease to function through life's many best laid plans gone awry, and wouldn't be who I am.

Thank you to Liza, for your guidance through the grief; you opened the gates for *Aria* and helped bring the "color back into my palette."

Thank you, most of all, to Dad. Thank you for loving us, your wisdom, your delight. Your refusal to be anyone but who you were. I hope you think it's "kewl" to have a paper-pushing villain with your name. Thank you for reading to us as kids. Thank you for creating your own adventures and leaving them on clipboards and notebooks around the house. Thank you for leaving a message where and when I needed to see it most. I sing no *Aria* without you.

I will meet you on the other side of Saturn, maybe a cozy spot in the Shire, for my long-overdue hug — someday.

ARIA FOR A GRASSHOPPER

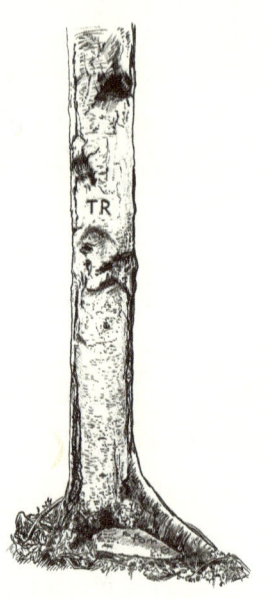

www.ingramcontent.com/pod-product-compliance
Lightning Source LLC
LaVergne TN
LVHW092013090526
838202LV00031B/2640/J